What Every Manager
Needs to Know About
MANUFACTURING

What Every Manager Needs to Know About MANUFACTURING

Richard G. Brandenburg, Editor

Excerpted from the
AMA Management Handbook, Second Edition,
William K. Fallon, General Editor

American Management Association

This book is available at a special
discount when ordered in bulk quantities.
For information, contact Special Sales Department,
AMACOM, a division of American Management Association,
135 West 50th Street, New York, NY 10020.

Library of Congress Cataloging-in-Publication Data

What every manager needs to know about manufacturing.

"Excerpted from the AMA management handbook, second
edition, William K. Fallon, general editor."
   Includes index.
   ı. Manufactures--Management. I. Brandenburg,
Richard G. II. AMA management handbook. 2nd ed.
HD9720.5.W38 1987   658   87-47714
ISBN 0-8144-7686-4

Printing number

10 9 8 7 6 5 4 3 2 1

Publisher's Note

The revised and expanded second edition of the *AMA Management Handbook*, originally published in 1983, is the single most comprehensive source of information on management available today. Over 1,600 pages long, the handbook contains 163 chapters, which are divided into fourteen major sections. Every conceivable management and business topic is covered.

Now, in response to numerous requests to make discrete sections of the handbook available to managers and executives with interests in specific fields, AMACOM Books takes great pleasure in publishing this excerpt, the complete section on manufacturing, as it originally appeared in the *AMA Management Handbook*.

This comprehensive volume provides indispensable information on every aspect of manufacturing—from strategies, planning, and processes to materials management, management information systems, cost reduction, and much more. It is our hope that this volume will prove as valuable as the original handbook has been to its thousands of readers.

Contents

MANUFACTURING STRATEGY

Manufacturing strategy is a dynamic set of management principles dictating how a product is manufactured, how resources are deployed in production, and how the infrastructure necessary to support manufacturing should be organized. Manufacturing strategy links the manufacturing function to the goals of business. This section describes a framework for the development of a manufacturing strategy.

Manufacturing in Business Strategy

To bridge the gap between business strategy and manufacturing strategy two basic tasks must be completed. Sources of competitive advantage in the business must be established, and the basic economics of the business must be analyzed. Figure 4-1 shows the crucial role that this information plays as a link between strategies. Completion of these tasks is a difficult, iterative process, but it is essential to the formulation of a successful manufacturing strategy.

Sources of Competitive Leverage

Real differences exist among competitors, and these differences cause different companies to achieve varying levels of profitability while competing in the same markets. Competitive leverage results from differences in marketing strategy, the ability of firms to focus on certain market/product niches, and the manufacturing technology employed, all of which influence the product quality/cost. Determining these differences is an important requirement for understanding competitive success factors for a manufacturing company. Understanding competitive dynamics, market demand, and the segmentation of the business is critical to the successful development of a manufacturing strategy.

A business segment is a set of products and customers that shares a common but distinct set of economics. Proper segmentation is crucial to determining where opportunities lie for establishing a competitive advantage through unique manufacturing missions for the different product segments. There are many ways to segment a business, but the only meaningful one is based on the real needs of the customer and the full product costs of meeting these needs.

The manufacturing missions address the specific manufacturing needs of the different business segments and set the direction for the appropriate manufacturing response. Fundamentally, the manufacturing missions help to resolve the following key issues: (1) What should be the scale, level of integration, and size of the plant? (2) Should the plant be product or process focused? (3) What should be the level of response capabilities to meet changing market needs? (4) Should the plant be situated near its markets or its supplier base? The resolution of these issues is essential to a manufacturing strategy and helps establish a company's competitive leverage primarily from a cost standpoint.

Business segments do not remain static but are in a constant state of flux, shifting with changes in customer requirements, company capabilities, competitor

Figure 4-1. Information links between business strategy and manufacturing strategy.

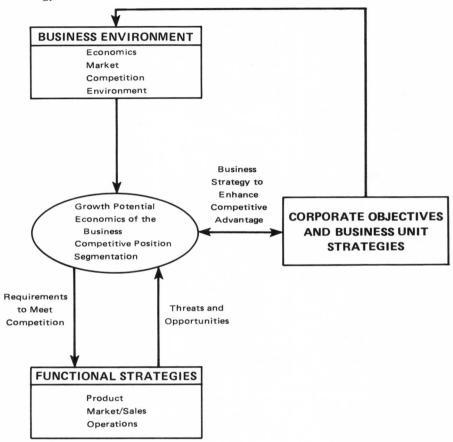

strategies and product/market focus, the economics of the business, and available technology. Thus a constant monitoring and reevaluation of the true business segmentation and the associated manufacturing mission requirements are essential to long-term success.

Economics of the Business

The process of segmentation necessitates an in-depth analysis of the economics of the business in two key areas: (1) the full costs associated with each product and the assets required to meet the end-user needs, and (2) the relation of these costs to changes in the environment.

Assessing the costs of meeting the end-user needs involves *all* stages of a product's life, from purchasing raw materials through production and distribution to the end of its useful life. The cost of raw materials, inbound freight, design and development, processing, packaging, engineering, distribution, marketing, and after-sales service must be broken out and analyzed in detail. For manufacturing strategy development, the analysis should focus on manufacturing costs including direct labor, plant and equipment, indirect labor, general expense, and overhead costs.

After the basic costs are determined, their movement with a changing environment over time should be analyzed. Plant scale, regulations, technology, segment focus, market share, product proliferation, and the labor climate are among the factors that affect manufacturing costs trends. Plant scale, for example, can affect manufacturing costs in two ways: it changes direct labor costs by affecting the number of employees, and it changes plant and equipment costs resulting from higher capital costs.

Market share, in the long run, can also affect costs. In a business in which market shares have been stable for some time, the relative accumulated experience of each competitor is virtually interchangeable with its relative market share. The competitor sustaining the leading market share accumulates the most experience and therefore has the lowest costs.

Product proliferation has a different effect on manufacturing costs. In mature markets, segments with different needs develop, and companies serving these markets will diversify to offer special products or services at a small premium. Typically, the leading competitor is the most able, and most inclined, to pursue new markets, because it can benefit most from economies of scale. The smaller competitor, on the other hand—with less experience, smaller share, and lower scale—maintains lower costs by running a more focused operation with fewer product offerings. Knowing the tradeoff between economies of total scale and product proliferation costs is essential to companies in these positions.

Key costs and the factors affecting them over time must be analyzed for each business segment. The analysis may lead to a redefinition of the business segments, and the process will be repeated. The business segmentation and associated cost structures which result from this process will be used to identify key areas in which business and manufacturing strategies have the most impact.

Manufacturing Strategy Techniques

Once the business segmentation is determined and key leverage points in the manufacturing cost structure are established, the groundwork for identifying manufacturing options exists. Some specific techniques for developing and understanding the available options are described below.

The Learning and Experience Curves

A learning curve exhibits the relationship between labor hours per unit and cumulative units produced. When this relationship is plotted using logarithmic scales, as in Figure 4-2, the result is frequently a linear relationship. Each time accumulated volume doubles, the labor hours per unit decrease by a set percent-

Figure 4-2. Relationship between labor hours per unit and cumulative units produced.

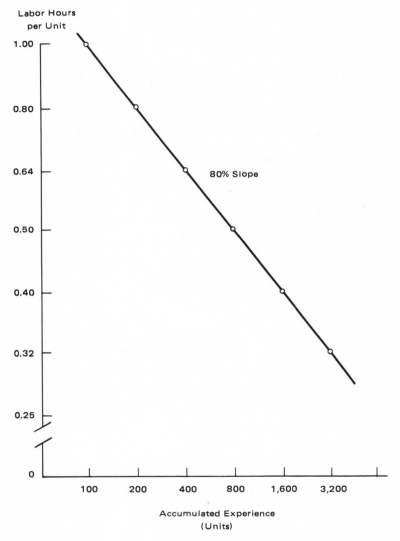

Accumulated Experience
(Units)

age. A 90 percent learning curve means, therefore, that when cumulative volume doubles, labor hours per unit are reduced by 10 percent to 90 percent of the previous level. The algebraic description of this curve is:

$$y(x) = ax - b$$

where $y(x)$ = direct labor hours required to produce x^{th} unit
    x = cumulative number of units produced
    a = number of hours required to produce first unit
    b = function the rate at which $y(x)$ decreases as cumulative
        production increases

The parameter b is a function of the rate of learning which occurs with each doubling of volume.

An experience curve is an expansion of the learning curve. Rather than relating cumulative volume to labor hours per unit, it uses total cost per unit. The unit costs used must be in constant deflated dollars, and must reflect *only* value added costs such as direct labor, indirect labor, capital costs, and overhead. They should not include such costs as purchased materials. Real unit costs typically decline 10 percent to 30 percent each time accumulated volume, or experience, doubles.

Many factors can influence the experience curve parameters. Technology advances, improved work methods, changes in batch size, and many other factors can combine with the basic learning process to shape the curve.

The competitive implications of the learning curve are important. If all industry participants compete in a similar manner, then the industry leader, who is accumulating experience fastest, will benefit most from experience curve effects over the long run. Therefore, industry followers *must* differentiate their products/services in order to achieve superior profitability. A good strategist attempts to profit from the experience curve effect in planning expansion, resource deployment, new processes, and other strategic actions.

Mapping Products to Processes

The relationship between product life cycle and process life cycle provides a framework for developing alternative product definitions and manufacturing strategy alternatives. Many products go through a three-stage life cycle. When the product is introduced, the market is small, changes in the product design are frequent, standardization is minimal, and the highest potential for gaining competitive advantage is to offer superior service. As the product matures, it becomes more stable, more standardized, and product quality/performance becomes the primary source of competitive advantage. Finally, the product becomes almost fully standardized, its market volume plateaus at a relatively high level, and competition is primarily based upon price. Products which do not pass through this cycle can be classified on the basis of product/market characteristics.

Intuitively, one can define the characteristics of the process technology required at each stage of the product life cycle. A new product requires manufacturing flexibility. A job-shop or general-purpose process best meets this requirement. The middle-aged product requires superior quality and room for innovation. A specialized or programmable technology is appropriate. The mature, standardized product must be dependable and must be produced at the lowest cost possible. This is achieved with highly automated and dedicated process technology.

A graph of product life cycle and process life cycle is shown in Figure 4-3. This two-dimensional matrix has many implications for the manufacturing strategist. Understanding the position of the company's current products on this matrix provides useful insights. For example: Do all products require the same level of technology? If not, should some products be redefined? Or should the process technologies employed be changed? Does the competition define their product in the same way? What competitive niche or position are they attempting to fill? What position should be assumed to meet the competition?

An attempt to position a new product on the matrix aids in developing strategic plans for capital investment and introducing the new product.

Figure 4-3. Chart of product life cycle and process life cycle.

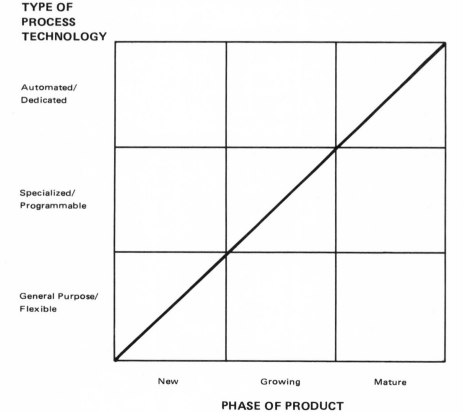

TYPE OF PROCESS TECHNOLOGY

Automated/
Dedicated

Specialized/
Programmable

General Purpose/
Flexible

New   Growing   Mature

PHASE OF PRODUCT

Focus and Complexity

In developing a set of strategic alternatives for deploying resources it is important to understand the relationship between products and processes within a facility. This understanding can be developed by examining product lines and the complexity of the processes required for their production.

A company with a few homogeneous product lines has simple production processes, and a company with a large number of products with divergent requirements has complex production processes.

A chart of product and operating complexity is shown in Figure 4-4. Each quadrant of the matrix defines a different combination of products and processes. An operation having a small number of process technologies is *process* focused, and an operation manufacturing similar products is *product* focused. When the numbers of products and technologies in a facility are both large it is said to be an all-purpose facility.

Figure 4-4. Product/process flow.

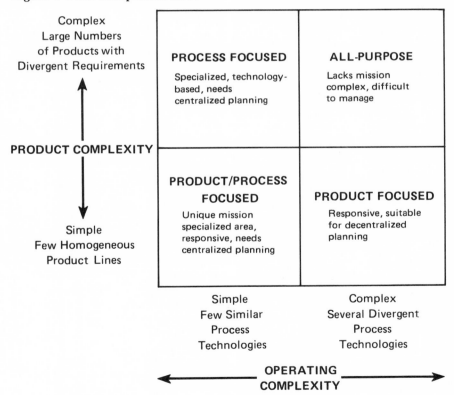

Each case has different implications. For instance, in an all-purpose facility several important strategic issues arise. Can the facility be separated into a number of smaller product-focused facilities? Process-focused facilities? Should the facilities be separated physically? Organizationally? How should the facilities be governed to meet the overall needs of the company? What are the infrastructure requirements?

All these techniques are tools identifying manufacturing alternatives and objectives. They should be used together with the analyses of competitive advantage and business economics to develop the manufacturing strategy.

The Manufacturing Strategy Framework

The operations strategy framework described here is illustrated in Figure 4-5. Notice that the focal point of the framework is the competitive and economic analysis leading to manufacturing mission for each product segment. This information feeds the search for manufacturing options, the analysis of manufacturing, distribution, and resource deployment issues, and finally, the development of a strategic plan. The entire process is of an iterative nature and its major elements are described below.

Product Segmentation

Product segmentation can be based on many different types of characteristics:

□ Product characteristics such as product range and position in life cycle.
□ Product/market characteristics such as product design, service needs, volume, margins, and demand variability.
□ Market strategy characteristics such as design leadership, cost reduction, diversification, innovation, and new-market entry.

After product segments have been chosen, competitive success requirements, such as price, quality, innovation, and service, should be identified.

Manufacturing Missions

A manufacturing mission describes the way a product should be sourced, manufactured, and distributed. It specifies levels of process flexibility, product mix, customer service, product quality, product cost, productivity, and other manufacturing requirements. Thus, the establishment of manufacturing missions ensures that product requirements for flexibility, lead time, quality, and cost will achieve a competitive advantage. They provide the strategic direction regarding (1) degree of process integration; (2) matching of products to technologies employed; (3) manufacturing management systems required; and (4) infrastructure to support production and distribution activities.

Response Gaps

A resource audit of current operations must be performed to establish a performance baseline and to uncover the real strategic operations issues. The audit will help identify places where current manufacturing response does not

Figure 4-5. Operations strategy framework.

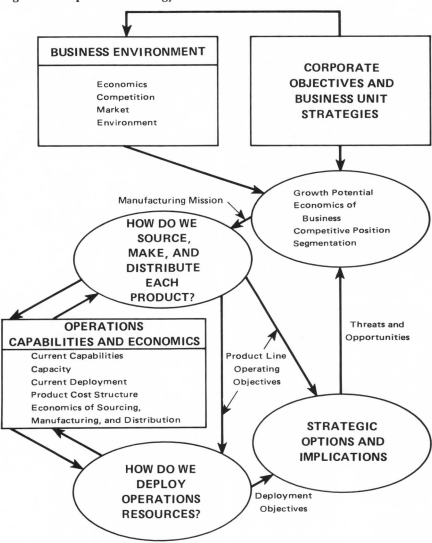

meet the product manufacturing missions. Several types of analyses are typically required in a strategic operations audit:

▫ A capacity analysis to identify the factors influencing capacity and its utilization. In particular, real future capacity shortfalls must be identified.

□ A product cost analysis examining product cost structures, direct labor productivity, materials costs, economies of scale, overhead costs, production
  yields, quality costs, distribution costs, and so forth.
□ A delivery performance analysis to discover service level shortfalls. Lead
  times required for procurement, production, and distribution should be
  specified.
□ An analysis of the amount of vertical integration and of the current process
  technology employed.
□ An analysis of the configurations and costs of competitors' operations.

Strategic Alternatives

Once the strategic audit is completed, the gaps between objectives and current response should be clear, and alternatives can be developed to close most
gaps. These alternatives can combine improvement opportunities in facility location and rationalization, means of product sourcing, manufacture and distribution, and organization structure and information systems employed to support that structure. The alternatives developed could move the business from
its present position to new positions with varying degrees of response improvement, new capital investment, and management structure and systems
changes.

Economic Evaluation

The evaluation of alternatives requires an analysis of the costs, benefits, and
risks associated with each alternative. The depth and coverage of the analysis
is likely to be less detailed than that required to support a capital expenditure
request, but it should be sufficient as the basis for a rational choice among the
strategic alternatives.

The alternatives chosen combine to create an operations plan, and the loop
has been completed. This plan becomes a part of the information in the pool
from which the process began, and will begin again and again as the environment changes. It establishes the framework for tactical planning and short-
term decisions regarding (1) investments in plant and equipment, (2) facility
expansion and consolidation, (3) manufacturing systems and controls, (4) manufacturing and distribution organization and structure, and (5) technology applications.

Case Example of Manufacturing Strategy Development

The following case history illustrates the application of the key elements in the
manufacturing strategy framework as well as some of the specific techniques
described. A pseudonym for the company is used to preserve confidentiality.

In early 1979, the management of Autoparts, Inc., a large manufacturer of
automotive components, was concerned about several aspects of its operation, including low productivity, particularly in its largest and oldest facility; uncompeti-
tive cost structure and margins; increasing competitive pressures from the largest

original equipment manufacturers (OEMs); and competition from European manufacturers that resulted in a loss of market share dating back to 1975.

In addition to these concerns, Autoparts was faced with mandatory product changes amd retooling because of downsizing needs, increased safety and environmental regulations, the prospect of a near-term downturn in the auto industry, and modest long-range growth.

To face these emerging threats, management set several major objectives: (1) maintain market position in its OEM product lines through a combination of cost reductions, retooling, and design changes to meet customer requirements; (2) improve customer service to enhance position in all product lines; and (3) improve long-term productivity of operations through selected investments.

Autoparts, Inc. had several product lines and served one dominant OEM customer and many smaller customers, including some in the auto aftermarket. Its manufacturing operations consisted of three facilities: a large and old facility in which a large number of products using several processes were manufactured; a second, more modern U.S. plant manufacturing one product line and specializing in machining and assembly; and a relatively small foreign facility that produced the full product line.

After gaining a thorough understanding of the business environment Autoparts faced, the next step was the segmentation of each of the company's product lines by key characteristics and success factors (see Figure 4-6). The competitive success factors for these product/market segments suggested three different manufacturing missions: (1) high degree of production flexibility and customer service for low-volume OEMs and aftermarket products; (2) product quality and process innovation for emerging medium-volume product lines for OEMs; and (3) lowest cost combined with high dependability of supply for products for OEM passenger car and light truck applications.

The manufacturing missions suggested different objectives in the areas of process technology, process integration, and management infrastructure for each of the three product/market segments. In Figure 4-7, these objectives and the current manufacturing response are illustrated for the three segments. The mismatch between product/market requirements and Autoparts' current response suggested strategic manufacturing alternatives that would then need to be further defined and analyzed for economic feasibility.

Autoparts' three manufacturing facilities were analyzed with a view to improving their productivity. Product and operating complexity were determined by using a strategic facility grid (see Figure 4-8). As a result, several alternatives for deployment were identified.

A detailed economic and feasibility study of specific technology, integration, operating systems, and new facility/redeployment alternatives resulted in a recommended long-range manufacturing strategy for Autoparts. Major recommendations included (1) investments exceeding $15 million in state-of-the-art process technology and increased integration for OEM product lines; (2) significant reorganization and redeployment among existing facilities for achieving a high degree of product and process "focus"; and (3) investments exceeding $6 million in U.S. satellite plants in a low-wage-rate region.

Figure 4-6. Product/market segmentation.

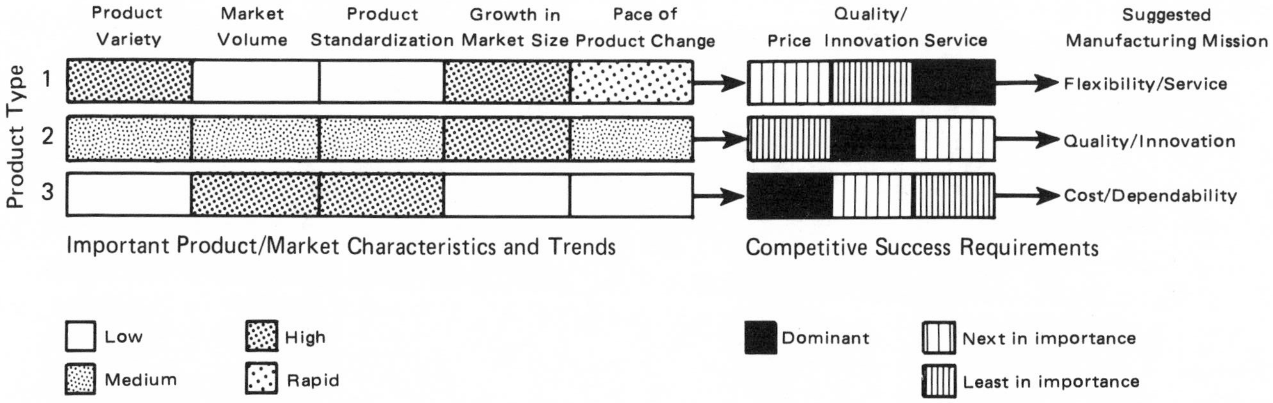

Figure 4-7. Strategic manufacturing objectives and alternatives.

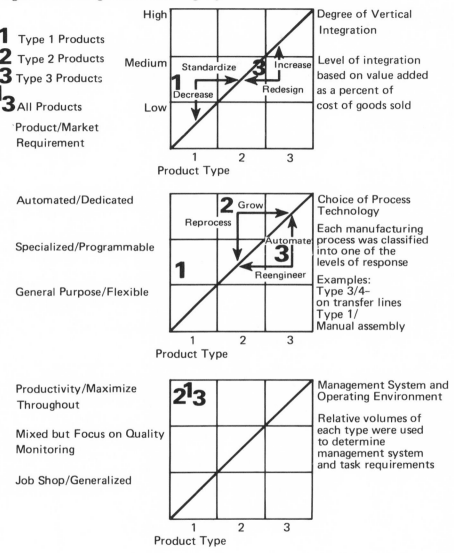

1 Type 1 Products
2 Type 2 Products
3 Type 3 Products
2¹3 All Products

Product/Market Requirement

Automated/Dedicated

Specialized/Programmable

General Purpose/Flexible

Productivity/Maximize Throughout

Mixed but Focus on Quality Monitoring

Job Shop/Generalized

Degree of Vertical Integration

Level of integration based on value added as a percent of cost of goods sold

Choice of Process Technology

Each manufacturing process was classified into one of the levels of response

Examples:
Type 3/4–
on transfer lines
Type 1/
Manual assembly

Management System and Operating Environment

Relative volumes of each type were used to determine management system and task requirements

Figure 4-8. Deployment objectives and alternatives.

Note: Facility is defined as an operating unit with a unified management structure, operating systems, practices, and policies

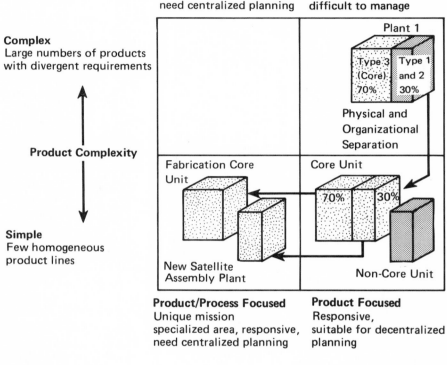

Process Focused
Specialized,
technology based,
need centralized planning

All Purpose
Lack mission,
complex and
difficult to manage

Complex
Large numbers of products
with divergent requirements

Product Complexity

Simple
Few homogeneous
product lines

Plant 1

Type 3 (Core) 70%   Type 1 and 2 30%

Physical and Organizational Separation

Fabrication Core Unit

New Satellite Assembly Plant

Core Unit

70%   30%

Non-Core Unit

Product/Process Focused
Unique mission
specialized area, responsive,
need centralized planning

Product Focused
Responsive,
suitable for decentralized
planning

◄———— **Operating Complexity** ————►

Simple
Few similar process
technologies

Complex
Several divergent process
technologies

Autoparts' new manufacturing strategy produced significant short-term and long-term benefits. Immediate benefits flowed from a decision to abort planned capital expenditures to expand existing facilities. Direct and measurable cost reductions were achieved through improved technology and reduced management complexity of current plants. When the new satellite plants become operational, Autoparts expects to become the lowest-cost producer in the industry. Because of its new way of thinking about and planning for its operations, Autoparts is now in a position to continue making long-term productivity gains in a dynamic and highly competitive environment.

Implementation Issues

The process of transforming a manufacturing strategy into an appropriate collection of plant, people, and policies is a difficult undertaking which requires resources, time, and management perseverance. The implications of the transformation are many, and here we touch on just two areas—business strategy and organizational issues.

Business Strategy Implications

Functional strategies, manufacturing strategies, and business strategies must work together to fulfill the corporate objectives. If they do not, then both the objectives and the strategies must be reevaluated.

The implications of the manufacturing strategies must be measured not only against corporate objectives but against potential response from the competition as well. Current competitive position and its direction should be evaluated in light of the chosen strategies and, again, adjustments should be made.

Organizational Issues

Organizational issues are rooted largely in the strategic choice between an all-purpose or a focused plant. These are essentially two extremes on the organization scale. At one extreme is the completely centralized facility. All processes and all products are lumped into a single plant. At the other extreme, each facility is a focused unit with responsibility for a single set of activities and objectives. In each of these cases a different organization is implied.

When all products and processes are housed in a single facility, little central coordination is required. Rather, responsibility can be spread down through the levels of the organization. When many focused plants are created, on the other hand, a large central organization is required to coordinate them, and less responsibility can be delegated to lower organization levels.

The organization structure also depends upon whether the facility is product or process focused. A product-focused facility is typically self-contained, and as such can operate as a profit center. The organization in such a facility can be highly decentralized, because each plant essentially operates independently from the other plants, and as a result is much more flexible. A process-focused plant, on the other hand, is typically one of several plants working together to produce a product. As such, it will likely be run as a cost center, and will be subject to the authority of a central coordinating unit.

Many other types of organization structures are possible. For example, a parts-making plant which supplies only one other plant may be operated as a satellite cost center with a skeleton staff on site, and with all other support coming from the main plant.

It is important to examine the implications of the chosen manufacturing strategies on the organization structure of the company, and to understand the kinds of changes which will be required for implementation of the strategies.

□ *Robert J. Mayer, Kush K. Agarwal, and Sara L. Beckman*

PLANNING MANUFACTURING ORGANIZATION

If there is a relative uncertainty about planning organizations, it stems from the many recent changes in the social-industrial environment that are affecting organizations. Illustrative changes in technology and attitudes are mentioned here for common background.

- Individuals who enter the workforce today have higher levels of educational and professional background, more open self-interest, and easier occupational mobility.
- U.S. success from 1950 to 1970 has dimmed our notice of other industrial systems that have gained at an increasing rate.
- The U.S. manufacturing "machine" has been in place too long—the average age of machinery and equipment is 25 or 30 years, and our plants are obsolete.
- The backlog of underused technology for productivity improvement includes numerically controlled machines, information systems, microprocessors, CAD/CAM, group technology, robotics, and genetic engineering.
- The number of informed buyers (the consumer movement) has grown.
- There is some return of cottage industries in handcrafted, artisan-type goods.
- Corporate "strategy" has been discovered, and research studies are available for efficacious and simultaneous consideration of product development, capital investment, and marketing sales programs in forward planning. This changes the impact of traditional functional goals on organization structure.
- Growing management requirements for obedience or conformity have spawned bureaucracy. Institutionalization has overtaken many organizations.
- Energy problems have changed manufacturing methods and equipment.
- There is growing dissatisfaction with adversarial relationships between unions and managers.
- Workers have become disenchanted with simplistic job definitions.
- There are more apparent needs for cooperative international development and use of the world's finite quantities of raw materials.
- Knowledge industries have grown.

- Population changes in the United States include an aging workforce.
- There are more shared responsibilities in our organizations, requiring managers to handle the differences between the "individual imperatives" and the "organizational imperatives" originally outlined by William H. Whyte.

These changes require new perspectives in planning manufacturing organizations for the 1980s.

Developing Strategies and Goals

Strategies and goals are prerequisites for organization plans because organization is a task-oriented system. Different kinds of organizations have to implement different kinds of strategies. Structure should provide for tradeoffs between the degree of coordination, speed of response, dependability of behavior, and amount and kind of information available. The organization structure should therefore relate to the range of possible actions and autonomy of decision making of the plant, department, or group.

Multiple products or markets or multiple profit centers in large corporations automatically restrict the potential strategies and affect organization plans considerably. Before the existing talent can be assigned tasks, roles, and accountability for parts of the total firm's activity, several conditions must be met: (1) The primary business/competitive mission has to be developed, (2) issues of capital/corporation productivity must be resolved and related to the values being added to the firm's operations, (3) product life cycles and new-product developments must be considered.

Primary Business Competitive Mission

The organization planner should determine which of these development stages the company is in:

Stable—making and shipping present product to the current market requirements; fine tuning may be required for profit improvement.
Growth-oriented and moving—new products, new materials; expansion required or in process.
Maintenance—limited growth and new-product development; mature, successful, cash flow, slow to change, little technology to consider.
Emerging—new, leading edge of new technology, small, entrepreneurial.

Having determined the development stage, the planner can begin to consider major tasks and the application of people to some of those tasks.

Capital/Corporate Productivity

Issues to be considered in planning total corporate productivity include the following:
Is a new plant required or can the old one be revised? (As substitute processes change production, much floor space is usually saved.)
Capacity changes require careful scrutiny in the 1980s. Inflation has caused

new equipment to be extremely high-priced while the cost of capital has grown three or more times over the preceding period. The cost of additional capital for additional capacity for midmature life cycle products, where learning curves have run out, is difficult to justify because unit production costs increase in the 1980s.

Machinery and equipment up-time are valuable assets. Utilizing close to 100 percent of the calendar time will provide the most return.

Working capital levels are affected by inventory. Planning operations to shorten work-in-process time by 33 percent are not difficult to achieve using finesse in scheduling, thereby lowering capital levels.

Energy currently represents approximately 10 percent of the total cost of production, and much reduction has occurred through conservation programs achieving as much as 50 percent savings.

Product Plan

Strategy as a determinant for organization planning should include the product plan related to the market. The issues to be considered include identifying the competitors' probable future plans, forces shaping total market behavior, and the product pricing policies currently being used. Strengths and weaknesses of competitors, their organization, and their products must be known in order to effectively block their programs.

Assigning People to Structures

If strategies and goals are important precursors to organizing, we cannot underestimate the effect of applying people to the tasks and structure of an organization. The growth of ponderous bureaucracies and overhead and "staff" employees producing more information, of which they use less, indicates that our organizations are less efficacious than they once were. (From 1978 to 1980 we added 600,000 blue-collar jobs and 5,500,000 white-collar jobs.) Background about the application of people to organizations should be reviewed before a specific chart or relationship is ordered.

Individual and Organizational Values

The mere act of publishing an organization chart does not create a staff of cooperating people. People may create incomplete systems of relationships, build structures without mutually accepted goals, and fail to function as promised. As any group of people interact, they instinctively feel pressures to organize their activities for efficiency. However, there are simultaneous pressures on individuals both to associate and to express themselves. Thus, conflicting objectives are generated for each person in the group.

Our Western ideals and political philosophy, however, support the idea that individual freedom to act exists or is enhanced when people willingly subordinate self-interest to social group or organization interests. This ability of members to subordinate self-interest is the central variable that managers must learn to handle in organization planning. These ideas meet a "frontier" spirit of self-reliance and independence. We seek to protect ourselves and our individualism, causing increasing difficulties for managers and increasing opposition to more "organization" in our lives.

These realities are in contrast to current exhortations to observe and to adopt other societal models. A role model being advanced for emulation is Japan, where centuries of confinement and isolation, with limited natural resources and land mass, have required intense collaboration for survival. Japan's outlook is much more holistic, whereas in the United States we resist becoming a series of true industrial families.

William H. Whyte discussed the inherent conflict of the individual and the organization in his book *The Organization Man* (Simon and Schuster, 1956).

Defining "imperative" as an implicit obligation or necessity, he outlined the needs of individuals and the needs of the groups as follows:

A	B
Individual Imperatives	*Organizational Imperatives*
innate nature of humans	malleability
individuality	obedience
indispensability	dispensability
community or generalization	specialization
spontaneity	planning
volunteerism	paternalism

When asked which they support, practicing managers unhestitatingly stated preferences for the values in column B. When asked to support their selections they stated that they admire the individual imperatives but they feel that the values in column B are more conducive to advancement within organizations.

Our changing culture and the relatively sluggish performance of our organizations require that we give some credence in the 1980s to these attitudes in structuring an organization today. The organization planner will be successful to the degree that he perceives the ways and the degrees that organizational imperatives (column B) have displaced the values of individuals in the organization being planned.

The successful arrangement of responsibilities, tasks, and duties into an organization plan will depend upon (1) how much obedience is essential to success in the organization's goals; (2) how much dispensability of people is necessary for the organization's adaptability to changes; (3) how much real specialization is required as opposed to generalization, and how sense of community can help for the organizational efficiency; (4) the degree of intervention of organization *planning* that is needed to reduce organizational uncertainty to achieve the organization's goals; and (5) how much paternalism justifies management's psychological dominion over the workforce to achieve the company's goals.

Scott and Hart indicate in *Organizational America* (Houghton Mifflin, 1979) that unfortunately the degree to which we deny our innate human nature may have already thrown open the door to domination of most Americans by organizational imperatives. They continue:

> Most of us in production and consumption mainstreams are inextricably involved in or committed to the organizational values. They are contemporary articles of faith that we must embrace if we expect to gain any rewards from the system that we have made for ourselves. They are the definition of organizational America.
>
> We made it so because we believe that the modern organization would provide us with material affluence, physical safety and peace of mind. We were not aware that we would be buying a whole set of new values or the extent that these new values would one day so directly affect our personal goals and satisfactions, nor the real success of the institution that we organized. . . . It is powerful. . . . We seem not to be able to escape. We cannot return to the simple life.

Therefore a manager must learn how to both maintain control and develop more faith in each person as he conceives the organization.

Power

Perceptions of power cause us to adhere to or circumvent the systematic interactions which are conceived at the time an organization is prescribed. The knowledge of the use and abuse of power is the most important tool in applying people to planning an organization. Management training literature does not treat the subject of power and its use in organizations, but it is an issue that should be considered with candor in discussions of organization planning.

According to Bruce D. Henderson in his book *Henderson on Corporate Strategy* (Abt, 1979), power as used in organization planning is defined as the "ability to initiate action and to disregard the initiations of actions by others." He goes on to say that "the first rule of power is to procure and compound it," by using rank order and territorial imperatives. Rank order is described as the pecking order, or the sequence in which managers accept initiating action from others. Territorial imperatives are defined as "the group's or species' territories"—the spaces, places, and functions that others would accept or recognize as the territory for a colleague's initiatives.

Persons who are skilled in the use of power or who have been placed in a position to exercise it may or may not develop leadership, which Henderson defines as the ability to choose and articulate the organization's conception of "ideal" performance.

The most important factors in an organization's success are the manager's values and style. In starting to build an organization's structure, then, a manager describes what an organization ought to do. The top manager sets the tone, the values, the goals, and the probable estimate of success and exercises leadership by motivating others to accomplish these ideals. The sure symptom of failure of leadership is when subordinates begin to say "the boss doesn't understand."

Management Styles and Structures

The manager's approach will probably reflect one of the three major styles:

- Autocratic—centralized information and centralized control, in a task-oriented organization with few decision makers. The decisions are communicated downward and the manager is not available for consultation with the organization.
- Paternalistic—a family concept, with a limited delegation of decisions and with goals set at the top; limited achievement is rewarded while too great achievement is considered menacing.
- Consulting style—a lot of information is available to everyone. There is an open climate, and there are interactive goals; decision making is very supportive of the people in the organization and their own initiatives at the lower levels.

Selection of one of these styles probably reflects the manager's attitude about the people to be organized and managed. In another discussion of personal style, Louis Barnes, of Harvard, has noted that trust is easily destroyed by adapting self-reinforcing attitudes of pervasive mistrust based on the manager's daily reactions to three natural and harmless assumptions.

The first one is that important issues naturally fall into two opposing camps, exemplified by either/or thinking. An antidote to this is to think "and/also" instead of "either/or."

The second assumption is that hard data and facts are better than soft ideas and speculation. This is exemplified in the idea that "hard drives out soft." (Managers support and defend their positions or changes with hard data. They act with defensive superiority and tough attitudes versus soft attitudes.) The antidote to this is a more appropriate attitude for leadership which conveys trust by portraying the ability to cope with new information, confront discrepancies, and show care for people and issues.

The third apparently harmless assumption is that the world is an unsafe place, and therefore managers are justified to hold a pervasive mistrust of the universe around them. The antidote is personal courage.

Too frequently, managers see these three ideas as healthy (thinking that only a fool would not be mistrustful in his particular situation of trying to make significant change). When managers combine all these three assumptions at the same time, which we do very naturally, there may be benefit in the short run, but it is usually very destructive in the long run.

In constructing an organization plan, consider the extent to which objectives for the organization can easily be adapted by subordinates and can fit the value schemes of various organization participants.

Concept of Shared Responsibility

Pressures are currently being applied by critics and theorists toward adaptations in participative management. Many responsibilities and much accountability for achieving objectives and realizing strategies are shared among a group, but the concept of shared responsibility is often overlooked in considering manufacturing cost problems.

All members of the group share parcels of the task to produce products and manage costs: The specs, tolerances, and performance characteristics of the product come from product design; the process that is used comes from manufacturing engineering; planned time and technical skills for the operators from the industrial engineers; climate and training from the supervisors; the manual skills are furnished by the operators themselves. In setting a total standard cost for the part or product and describing what activities are needed to meet planned costs, each function can influence the outcome by making decisions that are properly part of its specialized functional responsibilities.

Organization Typologies

There are five natural clusters or configurations in management structure, according to Henry Mintzberg of McGill University. Five general groups are placed within those structures: (1) the top management, called the *strategic apex;* (2) the basic workers in the organization, called the *operating core;* (3) intermediate managers who multiply the chief executive's efforts, called the *middle line;* (4) analysts and specialists concerned with formal planning and control of the work, called the *technostructure,* and (5) indirect service to keep all the other groups going— mailrooms, cafeterias, medical, legal, and so on—called the *support staff.*

Not all organizations are large enough or have complex enough requirements to put people is each of these responsibilities. However, the number and the extent of complexity follow the requirements for the work itself.

One of the five organization clusters is called the *simple structure,* which emerges when there is a direct order given from the chief executive officer (who is identified as the strategic apex) to the worker (the operating core). There are few line people to amplify the CEO's orders and little staff. This seems to fit when you have an innovative product, centralized control, and entrepreneurial characteristics, and when dynamic growth is under way.

A second classification is the *machine bureaucracy,* which is most prevalent when the enterprise is in a quest for, or in, mass production striving for, economy of scale. The enterprise contains all the elements of the goals of organizations: products are standardized, production systemization is elaborate, factories are horizontally decentralized, and middle management amplifies the authority of the top management and grows heavily.

The third kind of organization structure is *professional bureaucracy,* which usually describes such enterprises as hospitals, universities, accounting firms, and so on. A group of independent professionals, working democratically and using centralized skills, form this organization. There is a stable, complex environment of high-talent people; few changes in product take place, people get pigeonholed in jobs, and it is a true professional management bureaucracy.

A fourth group is called *divisionalized organization,* which is a loose coalition of several machine bureaucracies where each subunit is standardized like the organization in the machine bureaucracy.

Finally, there is an organization group called *adhocracy,* most familiar in aerospace and think-tank consulting group operations. Here we expect complexity and no standardization of technique. The structure remains fluid, shifting in emphasis and control among projects as different needs develop for collaboration among high-talent managers. There is a large operating core of high-talent people and loose support for the strategic apex.

The most conventional manufacturing organization chart, usually similar to the machine bureaucracy, is expected to look approximately like the chart in Figure 4-9.

Matrix Management

Corporate managers in a machine bureaucracy structure may create functional interest groups as teams when there are projects for particular products, services, or goals. Under these circumstances, participants have a line supervisor and a functional specialist supervisor. They are, in effect, reporting to different people in two different organization tracks. When these dual relationships are more permanent, the organization is described as a *matrix management* structure.

Quality Circles

Japanese management style and structures provide for worker-management groups that serve as project teams to improve output quality and relationships in their factories. A few American and Japanese companies have tried to replicate the system in the United States but with only modest success. Apparently the subordination of individual goals is not as attractive to U.S. workers as it is to the traditional hierarchical authority structures behind which stand centuries of social organization.

Studies of the Toyota workers, among others, indicate that the foremen still retain absolute authority in their departments. Moreover, in Japan the worker apparently never assumes that he can in any way challenge the decision-making power of his superior in his circle activity. Some research suggests that these circles of workers have roots in earlier attempts to minimize or diffuse the contribution of different individuals in the group.

Another factor that militates against the organizational use of small groups in the United States stems from the traditional adversary relationship between management and organized labor and from ethnic differences and pressures of the past. This background differs from the traditional apprenticeship system central to the evolution of the Japanese employer/employee relationship, which is based on the idea of industry as family.

However, consider the work processes of the maintenance employees whose efforts are usually unmeasurable and whose duties allow complete latitude in carrying out their tasks. Their work begins when order is interrupted, when unusual events take place. The difference in mode of operation between a maintenance employee and a product assembly-line employee highlights the essence of the problem of organizing. The individual imperative shows clearly here. While people become more developed themselves, the demand for order is tending to create a more defined role for the individual employee, with less for individual expression.

Figure 4-9. Conventional manufacturing organization chart.

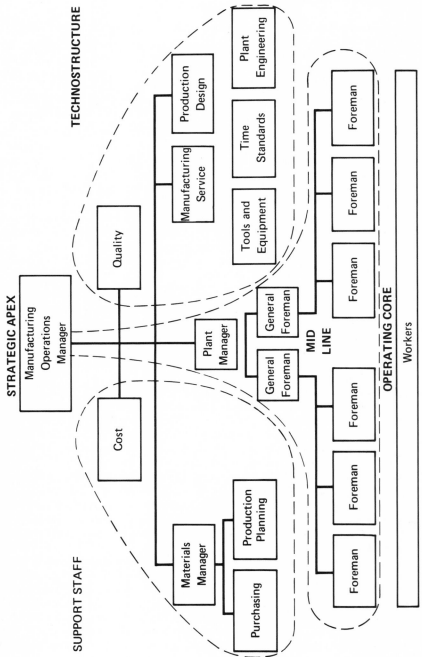

Span of Control

Span of control, which describes areas of accountability in an organization chart, is measured by the number of people reporting to a functional or executive position. Traditional limits have been established in organizations: the ideal is considered to be 6 managers with a maximum of 20 reporting. An organization reflects the abilities of its managers, their range of technical background, and their interpersonal skills.

Span of control requires a task with a clean start and a clean finish. A manager must describe the work content and the frequency of interpersonal contacts. There are usually minimum requirements for specific knowledge, and the critical nature of the content of the task should be described.

Delegation

Delegation is the way a manager parcels out or shares his own authority to act without his presence and/or timely acquiescence. Most managers accept accountability for functions and activities. Having determined that he cannot perform or manage all the tasks required to fulfill that accountability himself, the manager may decide to engage others to do the tasks or manage subgroups of people to perform them.

Once he has described the activity that he has assigned to another, he determines those duties and activities that his assignees (1) can act on without advising or asking others, (2) can act on but must report to designated persons about what they have done, (3) must ask about before they act, or (4) should await instructions before acting.

Informal Organizations

Research shows that the needs and requirements of individuals are so compelling that they manifest themselves through the formation of informal organizations or primary social groups within a company, a factory, or a large department. We have also learned that there are limits to what constitutes a group and that loyalty to the smallest unit objective is primary. This means that the plans of the plant or corporation are secondary to those of the small group.

An organization of more than 20 people cannot be considered one homogeneous body. The charts we use and the delegations of responsibility parceled out as tasks usually portray the organization as a series of smaller groups. Some smaller groups become social groups that provide real communication. Eight to ten people seem to be the critical number for face-to-face communication, and there is a tendency for groups larger than this to subdivide into smaller ones.

The small face-to-face group is the fact of life in any department or factory. C. I. Barnard writes in *The Social Psychology of Industry* (Penguin, 1980) that "the individual's deepest feelings take place within the bounds of this primary group of which he is a member. . . . He cannot, as it were, love, hate or feel other emotions at first hand towards the state, the army, the church, or a large company nor clash with those of his group." Therefore, if the worker (subordinate) feels that the interest of the firm clashes with those of his primary group, no amount of propaganda, pleading, or discipline will cause him to develop feelings of loyalty toward the firm.

Small primary groups are the instruments of society through which, in large measures, individuals acquire attitudes, opinions, goals, and ideals. They alone are fundamental sources of discipline and social control.

These observations find much support in the growth of quality circles adapted from Japan's industrial experience and evolving into participative management concepts in the United States. These groups are disciplined and exercise great peer pressure on attitudes and behavior.

Factories contain many informal organizations, frequently with objectives and structures entirely different from those of formal groups in the tables of organization. Structures that are in disagreement with these observations of human behavior or that break up such groups precipitate great social unrest.

Recognizing the dynamics of the human organization and the management of them, Machiavelli advised:

> And let it be noted that there is no more delicate matter to take in hand, nor more dangerous to conduct, nor more doubtful of its success, than to serve up as a leader in the introduction of changes. For he who innovates will have for his enemies all those who are well off under the existing order of things and only lukewarm supporters in those who might be better off under the new.

That was written in 1514 A.D. We sense that the major problems for modern managers still have to do with the dispositions of those persons whom we manage.

The test of the manager's ability to organize, therefore, is to get all the small social groups to subordinate their purposes to common goals of the firm, plant, or department.

Conclusion

Planning a manufacturing organization requires (1) knowing what the organizational goals and purpose are; (2) knowing the values that are to be the basis of accomplishing those goals; (3) understanding the economic environment for the organization and then deciding what strategies are to be used; (4) developing the relationship of the functions and describing an operations system; (5) understanding how people are expected to perform in the organization and communicating those expectations to subordinates; (6) previewing possible organization structures and selecting the most appropriate; and (7) describing tasks and planning to parcel out authority to minimize confusion in accomplishing those tasks.

□ *C. Eugene Moore*

MANPOWER PLANNING AND PERFORMANCE

The objective of manpower planning is to achieve the most effective and economical use of employee skills, efforts, and abilities in accordance with present and planned operating conditions.

Manpower Planning

Two basic factors in regard to manpower planning must be known in advance. They are the human skills required and the human skills available. Each must be measured in terms of the time available for productive use.

Required abilities. The skills and abilities required are determined by the nature of the manufacturing operation itself. There must be appraisal of available equipment, job methods, quality requirements, normal working conditions, and man-hours required to meet varying production schedules established from volume requirements and product delivery dates.

Availability of skills. The skills and abilities available must be determined by evaluating and appraising the employees in terms of available skills, knowledge, physical abilities, and job responsibilities.

Man-hours required. The man-hours of abilities required are determined from job process sheets, productive job standards, measured nonproductive work, labor variance data, production requirements (per order and per period), available equipment, and delivery schedules.

Job process sheets describe the operations sequences on the tools and equipment required.

Productive job standards, when multiplied by the volume requirements, establish the productive labor time needed. The addition of the predictable measured indirect labor hours (such as setup, machine maintenance, and so forth) and the percentage of time required for nonproductive labor variances resulting from waiting for work, training, temporary methods allowances, and similar factors will determine the expected man-hours required at a normal performance level.

The required man-hours can be established by operation, cost center, department, or machine. These in turn can be easily expressed in terms of required skills and abilities to the same degree of accuracy.

Man-hours available The man-hours of skills and abilities are described in the job evaluation plan, payroll earnings efficiencies, and employment records.

The job descriptions of the job evaluation plan should describe the job requirements, provide an employee performance efficiency list, and state the potential improvement to be expected over and above the schedule developed from the job standards. Employment records will indicate available skills not in active use which may be saved for emergency or peak periods.

The man-hours of available skills can be determined by multiplying the number of employees who have the required abilities by the working hours available on the particular machine or in the work center, department, or plant.

Problem analysis and solutions. Planning and administering a manpower plan and schedule are carried out as in operating a straight-line, paced conveyor system. But here it becomes apparent that perfection in balance can never be achieved; it can only be approximated. In scheduling manpower, there is always a bottleneck or critical position which limits or restricts every other phase. The major bottlenecks encountered in manpower planning and scheduling are a critical machine or process, a limited number of specific job skills, limited facilities and space, and uncontrollable production requirements. It is obvious that a manpower scheduling plan designed to improve the complete function must concentrate on minimizing the effect of any bottlenecks indicated by preplanning and analysis.

Minimizing bottlenecks. The most common methods of minimizing the effects of manpower bottlenecks are overtime; extra shift operations; scheduling of longer runs to minimize lost productive time caused by setups, job changeover, and the like; provision of relief operators; methods and job improvement; and wage incentives. Decisions as to which of these solutions is most effective are based on tangible economic considerations, available personnel, and—in some instances—labor-management agreements.

The additional cost of overtime can be readily calculated and evaluated in terms of its effect on product cost. The addition of an extra shift can be considered in terms of the available personnel who are capable of handling the operation and in terms of the increased operating expenses caused by extra supervision and staff personnel required. The use of longer runs per job order can be evaluated in terms of added inventory costs, additional storage space requirements, and the increase in invested capital requirements. The use of relief operators to provide greater use of productive machine time necessitates consideration of the available qualified personnel and the added labor cost. Increased job efficiency and performance created by means of job methods improvements and an effective wage incentive plan are obvious answers to the improvement of productivity and the operation of manpower planning and scheduling systems. If an effective wage incentive system is in operation, the major portion of the technical details necessary for the development of a sound system is already available.

Many manpower bottlenecks are caused by unique operations or machines requiring long learning times. These are inevitably long, complex operations. Frequently, such operations can be broken down into a series of less difficult operations which are easier to learn and require simple tools and machines. While the ultimate labor cost for the series of operations may be greater than that of the original complex task, the effect on productivity and reduced unit cost may be sufficiently great to justify the increase in direct labor cost.

In many seasonal industries, the characteristic job skills are required for only a portion of the year. To hire skilled help for seasonal work is difficult under most situations and almost impossible during periods of labor shortage; furthermore, such practices usually involve major expense for hiring and training. Careful consideration should be given to evaluating these costs and comparing them with the costs of maintaining a stable, year-round force that may on occasion be called upon to perform make-work duties. Properly planned, these make-work occupations can produce results valuable in the overall administration of the business.

Wage Incentives

A wage incentive plan is a wage payment system that offers employees an opportunity to increase earnings by better-than-expected performance.

Economic Value

The economic value of incentives to management and labor is widely recognized. The accompanying tabulation summarizes the production increases that can be expected from the application of a sound and effective wage incentive system to work currently paid on a nonmeasured day-work basis. (These findings apply to labor-controlled operations only.)

	Type of Production		
	Highly Varied	*Varied*	*Mass-Produced*
Average expected production increase	105%	80%	47%
Average reduction in unit direct labor costs	40	30	20
Average reduction in unit overhead costs	80	70	60

It is of course equally important to consider the losses that will be suffered by improper operation of a wage incentive system. Experience indicates that such losses may result from improper rate setting, faulty time-keeping, inaccurate piece counting, arithmetic errors in documentation, unmeasured work performed by incentive operators, and improper control of incentive plans.

Where a moderately effective wage incentive plan has been in use, its abandonment in favor of a nonincentive wage system has been found to have the effects shown in the following tabulation. (These figures are applicable only to labor-controlled operations rather than those controlled by equipment or processes or where wage limitations on incentive earnings have been in effect.)

	Expected Loss of Production	
Type of Work	*With Measurement and Control*	*Without Measurement*
Highly repetitive	36%	43%
Semirepetitive	44	58
Nonrepetitive	47	59

Motivation

The key words in the definition of wage incentives are "opportunity" and "motivate." An incentive system that, on the contrary, is based on real or imagined penalties rather than opportunities is usually ineffective, for it is rarely accepted and operated with the full cooperation of the employees. In fact, a major problem in gaining the acceptance and use of wage incentive plans is the widespread opinion that incentive systems penalize and restrict rather than offer additional opportunities.

To motivate employees, an incentive system must meet the following criteria: (1) the earnings opportunities must be sufficiently attractive; (2) the basis and the methods used for determining the rewards must be understandable and acceptable to the employees; (3) the rewards must be considered as commensurate with the extra efforts and abilities expended by each employee; and (4) the employees must be protected against conditions beyond their control. Unless every aspect of the wage incentive system meets these criteria, it will not function properly.

Opportunity

The attractiveness of the wage rewards is inevitably measured by employees in terms of possible addition to their total pay; therefore, the earnings opportunity must exist in (1) the performance standards themselves and (2) the percentage of incentive opportunity available during the total pay period.

The average earnings opportunity for a good incentive performance based on measured standards should be at least 25 percent over the day-work earnings level. Thus an employee working completely on measured standards could expect to increase his pay by that percentage by providing a good incentive performance for the full period. It should be emphasized, however, that 25 percent is the average expected opportunity. As individual skill and effort vary, so will individual earnings potential.

No limits should be placed on incentive earnings; limited opportunity will result in limited performance. Many people have exceptional operational skills; they should be encouraged to use their talents to their fullest capacity and should be rewarded for them.

Adequate incentive opportunities must also be available. Even though the performance standards themselves offer a provable 25 percent incentive opportunity, the total earnings potential for a pay period may be insufficient to motivate the employee if too few hours of incentive work are available. For example, if only 20 percent of the hours worked by the employee offer incentive opportunity, his potential payment earnings through the incentive plan will be only 5 percent greater than his guarantee.

Employee Acceptance

Each incentive employee must fully understand the principles, policies, and practices of the incentive system if he is to accept it, have confidence in it, and be motivated by it. Lack of understanding will result in unavoidable malpractices, earnings inconsistencies, and operational errors which, in turn, will destroy confidence in the incentive plan and lead to its inevitable destruction.

An employee who works on the incentive system must thoroughly understand how his incentive standards are set; the method to be followed in order to meet and surpass the standards and produce a quality part; and the responsibilities and activities covered by the standards, as well as those that are not included. And, finally, he must be able to calculate his incentive earnings in order to verify the accuracy of his incentive pay.

Each of these requirements is of vital importance. For example, the incentive standard is usually based on a specified job method that must be followed if the standard is to be valid. If the proper method is not followed, the standard may not be achievable and/or the quality may be improper. In either event, the employee's earnings will suffer.

Job incentive standards seldom—and should not—include allowances for unpredictable, substantial variations. When such variations from normal conditions occur, they must be compensated for, over and above the established standard. If they are not, the employee's incentive earnings will be adversely affected. If the employee knows what is and what is not included in the incentive standard, these variances can be brought to the supervisor's attention when they occur, and temporary allowances or adjustments can be made to compensate for the unavoidable condition. Hence the incentive opportunity will always be available and the motivation provided by the incentive system will continue to exist.

It is equally important that the employee be able to determine, by personal calculation, how effectively he is operating and earning. He is thus in a position to check and verify the pay he receives and to determine how well he is doing at any particular time during the pay period. This, in turn, lends further stimulus and motivation to increased performance.

Individual Performance

The incentive opportunities offered by a wage plan must be understood and accepted as being commensurate with extra performance. This relationship can be easily recognized if the incentive system is applied to individual performance, for an employee working on an individual incentive fully realizes that his earnings are a direct and personal reward for his own efforts and are not shared with or provided by others. Consequently, the greatest incentive pull exists when the incentive is applied to the individual employee.

Productivity Standards

The most widely used incentive plans are based on productivity. For such plans, a standard of productivity is established that can be met by a qualified operator working at a normal or day-work level of effort. Performance standards are usually expressed in terms of money, time, and/or number of units produced. Standards so established can be exceeded when the operator exerts better than normal skill and/or effort.

Piecework.   If money standards are used, the incentive system is known as piecework. Under a piecework system, the standard of performance is expressed as dollars or cents per unit produced, such as 2 cents per piece or $2 per 100 pieces. The employee is paid this fixed amount of money for the total number of units produced in one day's time. Under a piecework plan, the employee's earnings increase in direct proportion to his production. The unit labor cost is constant for normal or better than normal performance.

Standard hour system.   A variation of piecework is the standard hour system. Here the basis for performance is the standard hours or time allowed to produce the unit or product. To calculate incentive earnings, the units produced by an employee are multiplied by the standard allowed hours per unit. The result is the standard hours earned by the employee. These hours are then multiplied by the employee's hourly rate of pay, thus determining his incentive earnings. The standard hour system, like piecework, provides a fixed unit labor cost for normal or above-normal performance. Thus an employee's earnings increase in direct proportion to his productivity.

There are many variations of the basic standard hour incentive system; usually, they have been designed and installed to compensate for measurement and/or incentive control problems or to provide a strong incentive to meet and surpass the normal performance level. The Halsey and Rowan plans are typical of the first of these variations. They are used primarily where the time standards are estimated and unrefined or where close control of manufacturing variance cannot be maintained.

The Gantt task and bonus plan and the standard time performance plus plan are variations of the basic piecework and standard hour systems. Both offer a strong additional incentive to meet the established performance levels at which the direct incentive begins.

Halsey plan.   The Halsey plan shares the time saved between the employee and the company; hence, excessive earnings resulting from very liberal standards are minimized. Earnings are calculated according to the following formula:

$$[\text{Time taken} + F (\text{time allowed} - \text{time taken})] \times \text{hourly rate} = \text{earnings}$$

F, the incentive factor, is usually .5, but other values can be and are being used.

Rowan plan.   The Rowan plan offers a bonus on the amount of time saved. The theoretical maximum saving in time is, of course, 100 percent or twice the guaranteed earnings. The formula used is as follows:

$$\left[\text{Time taken} + \text{time taken} \left(\frac{\text{time allowed} - \text{time taken}}{\text{time allowed}} \right) \right]$$
$$\times \text{hourly rate} = \text{earnings}$$

Gantt plan.   Under the Gantt plan, a low guaranteed rate is offered for substandard performance. Upon achievement of the normal performance level, a higher hourly rate of pay is awarded, becoming the basis for the calculation of all above-normal incentive earnings.

Standard time performance plus plan.   A higher hourly rate of pay is offered under the standard time performance plus plan than under the Gantt plan. The minimum rate is usually the going rate for the proper class of work in the area. A more moderate bonus, up to 10 percent, is offered for achieving and surpassing the standard. Once standard performance is achieved and surpassed, incentive earnings are calculated at the higher day rate. In both systems, unit labor cost is calculated at the higher of the two rates.

These plans and various modifications of them have been employed where a substantial increase in productivity is required in order to meet the properly established performance standards. The additional bonus makes such plans more appealing to employees because it rewards them for the initial increase in productivity necessary to reach the level at which the incentive pay begins.

It should be emphasized that an infinite number of mathematical formulas can be used; most of the existing formulas have been tailored to meet a particular set of conditions. However, with the increased accuracy and availability of new and effective wage control techniques and procedures, the administrative and technical shortcomings of the past that made necessary these variations to the basic standard hour incentive system have been eliminated or at least minimized.

Group Incentive Systems

The various wage incentive plans described above are most often used for individual wage incentives. However, operating conditions frequently make the use of individual incentives impractical. Where this is true, a group payment plan may be advisable or necessary. If so, it is equally applicable.

A group incentive system is a system applied to a group of employees working in a common geographic location, on a related type of work, or on an interrelated activity. Its basic purpose is to enable those participating in the group to pool their efforts and performance and then equitably share the incentive earnings of the group.

One such application is made to paced conveyor lines or machine-controlled operations in which the production is controlled by the equipment. The group system gives employees on such work an opportunity to share the work and share equitably in any incentive earnings. A second instance in which a group incentive system is useful is in its application to activities, such as heavy maintenance of construction tasks, where a group of craftsmen may handle a major assignment collectively. In such instances, it is impractical—if not impossible—to specify, measure, and control the individual job assignments; hence, the total job must be measured in terms of labor content, and the detailed sharing of the work is determined by the employees on the job. A third instance is a short-run machine group, in which the greater part of the work of each employee is composed of setup time, machine attendance, troubleshooting, and the like, making it impossible to establish and control a specific method and a precise standard for each individual employee.

The determination of efficiency (incentive) earnings is the same for a group system as it is for an individual incentive plan. The time earned by the group is determined by multiplying the established standards by units produced. Extra allowed time, such as waiting for work, is added to the group incentive time earned. The total earned hours thus determined are divided by the hours worked by the group members to determine a group efficiency. Each group member's pay is calculated by multiplying his individual hours worked by his individual hourly rate and multiplying the result by the earned group efficiency.

Wherever possible, groups should be limited to 15 or fewer employees in order to make the individual incentive motivation direct and recognizable to each and all. Under the proper conditions, the group system will provide a highly practical and effective method, satisfactory to employees and company alike, for paying labor incentives.

Overall Bonus Plans

There is an infinite variety of overall bonus plans based on productivity, profits, savings, and/or combinations of the three. Examples are the well-known Scanlon plan, the Kaiser plan, and similar systems which are, in effect, profit-sharing arrangements. (Excellent source material describing many of these plans in detail is available.) It is imperative, however, that a plan of this type truly reflect the problems and conditions in the plant or company to which it is to be applied.

Problem Areas

Contrary to popular belief, incentive systems do not police themselves. They must be carefully established and even more carefully maintained by constant audits and checks if they are to remain effective. If these precautions are not taken, the systems will quickly deteriorate, and as a result serious labor relations problems and equally serious cost problems will result. The major problem areas encountered in wage incentive operations are inconsistency of standards, improper control of job variances, and inadequate incentive coverage. Each of these problem areas contributes to the deterioration of the others; unless they are constantly policed, the incentive system will deteriorate. When deterioration occurs, its effects on other important areas of management can be—and usually are— more serious than the obvious labor relations problems created.

If the incentive standards are inconsistent, their use for machine scheduling, departmental manning, production planning, inventory control, and the like will create serious errors. The standard costs of given products (if based on inconsistent production standards which are part of the incentive system) will be equally inconsistent, resulting in equally serious effects on pricing, profit determination, and marketing policies. They will also result in erroneous decisions in purchasing, equipment selection, plant layout, and the like.

A wage incentive system properly established and maintained is one of management's best assurances of the validity of the basic information it must use in most of the management functions and activities. Since employee earnings are directly in question, a constant check of standards and variance control is maintained throughout the organization. Hence, wage incentives properly used are a most valuable tool of management, serving many other activities as well as employee motivation.

Standards Maintenance

To develop and continue to maintain consistent standards, the following conditions must exist: a consistent technique for setting all standards; production standards based on specific, predescribed job methods and quality standards; an established, acceptable procedure for changing standards that are affected by creeping methods changes and employee job improvement suggestions; and a sound wage structure based on an acceptable and consistent job evaluation or job-ranking system.

Predetermined motion times and proven standard data developed from accurate, individual time studies are by far the most effective techniques for establishing production standards. Both methods require the predescription of the method and quality conditions, and the standards developed from them are based on massive data which more truly represent the so-called normal or average performance level.

Regardless of the rate-setting procedure used, the production standards themselves should cover only the predictable conditions and variations of the task. Any attempt to broadly average unpredictable variations into the published standards will result in a wide fluctuation of earnings, depending primarily on the existence or nonexistence of the variances which have been averaged into the rates at a particular time.

Proper definition of the method and quality standards on which the production standard is based is mandatory, for productivity variations resulting from methods changes and/or short-cutting quality requirements are the major single cause of variation extremes in performances and variances. When such extremes occur, the employee's concept of a fair standard is inevitably based on the highest figures. If tangible evidence of the basis on which the standard was set is unavailable, mutually agreed-upon solutions are difficult if not impossible to achieve.

The part played by creeping methods changes in the destruction of wage incentive systems is well known. Merely minor changes may be insufficiently important to warrant immediate changes in the existing standard. However, a series of such minor changes caused by working conditions, minor material changes, equipment improvement, and the like over the years create loose or inconsistent standards—or both—and an ineffective wage incentive is the inevitable result.

The production standards and related incentive administrative procedures may be established with accuracy and consistency, but an incentive system will still not function properly unless equally accurate and consistent controls for variations in manufacturing conditions are in existence. Such variances (which may come from a multitude of causes—temporary material variations, waiting for work, temporary methods, and the like) must be measured and allowed for, over and above the published standards. To control such variances it is imperative that an equally factual measurement procedure be available so that time standards can be set for these unusual conditions before or during their occurrence. Variances that are unpredictable (waiting time, for example) must be measured and controlled by an accurate timekeeping system that will enable the time variances to be measured and allowed for with equal accuracy. A third and final control required is accurate piece counting or production determination. These activities must be established as simple, verifiable procedures accurately reflecting the true amount of work done. If they are not, the wage incentive system will fail.

Making the Decision

A decision to introduce a wage incentive system, modify an existing wage incentive system, or abandon a wage incentive system must be predicated on a tangible, factual appraisal of existing productivity, costs, and administrative considerations. Such an examination (audit) must be an in-depth study that considers the specific details rather than a broad overall evaluation of productivity and costs.

Appraising Productivity

The audit should begin by establishing tangible and provably consistent production standards for selected operations. These standards may be developed by any accurate and accepted system of industrial work measurement. Predetermined motion time standards and provable standard time data derived by time study are usually the most effective work measurement tools for this action.

The operations selected for the evaluation should statistically represent the distribution of operations and skills applied in the factory.

By the use of accurate test standards, a direct comparison can be made between existing productivity and actual production studies taken on the floor with a consistent norm. The deviations will indicate the degrees of difference between actual and expected normal production and unit labor costs, where they exist, and in most cases the causes of the variations.

The production and time variances over and above those allowed for in the production standards can be determined by several methods: ratio delay studies or examinations of company records of downtime, lost time, waiting time, losses due to defective material, and the like.

Appraising Administrative Techniques

Equally important are the evaluation and appraisal of the administrative techniques used or required and the acceptance of the wage incentive plan by supervision, the bargaining unit, and the employee. An in-depth appraisal of this phase would cover the following areas:

- The technical aspects of establishing time standards would be studied with the objective of determining the adequacy and consistency of this basis for the most critical controls of management.
- The qualifications of the personnel responsible for the time standards would be appraised to determine their ability to use the required techniques properly.
- The acceptance of wage incentives by labor and management would be weighed to determine existing or potential sources of labor relations problems and evaluate possible solutions.
- Wage incentive controls would be appraised to determine inconsistencies which might result in disrupting time standards, costs, earnings, or management controls.
- Management control data would be appraised to determine the quality and quantity of information available to the management team for its assistance in maintaining a sound and effective wage plan, and to determine the effectiveness with which these data and reports are used to control costs, to utilize equipment, and to fairly and equitably administer the wage plan.

Each of these areas should be subjected to thorough investigation through a cooperative study by all who are engaged in the wage incentive operation. An evaluation or ranking procedure should be developed and applied in order that the appraisal be conducted as a fact-finding and educational procedure.

The audit, properly developed, will indicate the problem areas, their magnitude, and the steps necessary for their correction; the course of action which should be pursued for the mutual advantage of management and employees; and the economic justification for the necessary actions.   □ *John L. Schwab*

MANUFACTURING PROCESSES

Functional manufacturing activities start when a product design is to be manufactured. The design of the product commits the production system to specific processing methods because it designates the materials (raw, purchased, finished), the manufacturing or conversion processes (tools, layout, and so forth), the operation sequences, and the labor and skills required. Costs are set by the design, and therefore constant vigilance is required to correlate the design and the manufacturing process planning to ensure that elements of the design are economically appropriate.

There are three techniques in the surveillance of the design that can be used to moderate the costs: (1) value analysis and engineering, (2) group technology, and (3) tolerance and specification control for manufacturing.

Value Analysis

Value analysis (sometimes referred to as value engineering) basically consists in (1) analyzing and evaluating the fundamental use of a product; (2) systematically attempting to build greater value into the product without reducing its performance or interfering with its function; and (3) simultaneously reducing its cost. The principles of value analysis should be applied at the drawing board when a product is initially designed (sometimes referred to as "first look"), and continued all the way through each of the operations to final assembly. In the past, the techniques of value analysis were frequently used not on new products but primarily on existing products. When these same techniques are applied to existing products and product lines, they are referred to as "second look." Second look should be used as a supplement to—not a substitute for—first look. Although specific techniques vary from industry to industry, the goal is to increase the difference between the product worth and product cost, thereby increasing the value to the customer.

Need for value analysis.   The need for wider use of value analysis has never been greater, since competition is growing fiercer and customers are demanding better quality products at lower prices. Because value analysis attacks the cost-and-value problem from a functional standpoint, thereby getting to the root of the problem, it is well suited to helping meet the customers' needs.

Organizing for value analysis.   The goal in organizing the value analysis program is to bring the right people together at the right time on the right product. Participation and endorsement by top management are vital, because the program is based on new perceptions and knowledge from many departments, including the purchasing, marketing, design engineering, manufacturing, cost, and field service functions. Management could gather experts from many different disciplines, utilize their combined creative ideas, and end up with a lower-cost, superior product.

The organization of the function depends upon many factors such as the type of product and customer and the size and organization of the company itself. Reporting should be to a key individual high enough up in the chain of command so that a corporate viewpoint is maintained, prompt decisions can be made, and implementation can be rapid. When value analysis is a centralized function, the overall responsibility often rests with a corporate officer who is frequently chosen because of his specialty and the overall orientation of the company (for example, a vice president of engineering if the company is engineering-oriented). When value analysis is a noncentralized function, the overall responsibility often rests with a divisional manager.

Aid to purchasing. Since materials frequently make up the highest percentage of the total cost of an item, value analysis can be particularly valuable in purchasing. The cooperation of suppliers can be encouraged by the use of incentive contract clauses that enable them to share in any savings that result from their recommendations on such things as standard parts, loosened tolerances, design changes, or the substitution of less expensive material.

Evaluating results. Value analysis programs are difficult to measure quantitatively. One method of measurement compares the estimated savings in labor and material with the estimated cost (including costs of redesign, tooling, and analysts' time). However, there may be additional intangible savings, such as increased reliability or improved quality, which cannot be quantified. Any evaluation of the overall effectiveness of the program must be done carefully and objectively, taking into account all related factors.

Group Technology

We have learned from the Machine Tool Task Force Committee that their users are approximately 80 percent batch and piece manufacturers, not high-volume parts makers. The idea that most American manufacturers are high volume is not correct.

Many products within a company have similar parts and use similar processes. Once recognized, these similarities can be a powerful tool for organizing the production process and reducing costs. European managements named this concept of similarity *group technology*. The Machinability Data Center, a department of Defense Information Analysis Center, defines group technology as a manufacturing philosophy based on the recognition of similarities in the design and manufacture of discrete parts. The usual tendency is to consider each manufactured part as unique, since a casual visual examination of a total part population does not usually reveal commonalities. However, parts can be categorized into groups or families if their fundamental attributes are identified. An example of such a parts family is shown in Figure 4-10.

Through the systematic classification and grouping of parts into families on the basis of their design or production similarities, significant cost reductions can

Figure 4-10. A family of parts.

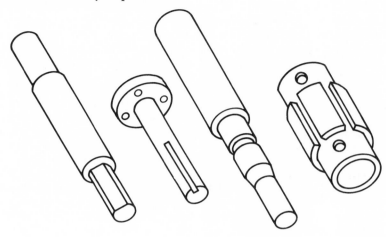

be achieved. Parts classification is a necessary activity in group technology systems and can be accomplished using one of a variety of classification and coding schemes.

Group technology is an approach that attempts to obtain the economic benefits achievable with mass-production techniques in those industries that are characterized by batch or job-shop manufacturing. Its recognition, application, and acceptance are rapidly increasing, because it offers industry an alternative in the face of economic pressures. A number of the techniques of industrial organization associated with group technology have been practiced by progressive companies in the United States for many years, and the evolution and coalescence of these methods in recent years has been remarkable.

By the turn of the century, F. W. Taylor had already introduced the use of mnemonic classification, which embodied some of the concepts of what we now call group technology. In the early 1920s, the Jones and Lamson Machine Company built machine tools employing principles of product standardization, product rather than process department allocation, minimal routing paths, and visual control of work. Over the years these and other approaches were refined and called by a variety of names (for example, part family manufacturing), but group technology was not recognized or practiced on a widespread basis in those industries characterized by small-lot production.

The scope of group technology is broad. Since its inception it has been associated with part family manufacturing and has been considered to affect all areas of a manufacturing company including design, process planning, manufacturing, assembly, and so on. It should also be noted that group technology applies both to mass production where the approach of fixed automation (for example, transfer line machines) is used and to small-lot discrete-parts manufacturing. In the typical manufacturing plant the excessive setup time, caused by the product mix and small lot sizes, may be the most significant part of the total production time. Furthermore, plants typically have a functional layout of equipment; consequently, jobs take a nearly unpredictable path through the plant in order to reach all the necessary processing locations. Production scheduling and production control become very complicated, and actual information on the status of any particular job is nearly impossible to obtain.

Group technology alleviates mass confusion by first grouping parts into families having manufacturing similarities. In this way different parts requiring similar machines and tooling may be processed in a sequence that increases the quantity per setup, thereby significantly reducing setup times and costs. Machines used in the production of similar part families are grouped together forming a machine group or cell (hence the name "cellular manufacturing"). This layout has the effect of reducing the scope of the problems of production scheduling, production control, materials handling, and so on, and at the same time tends to improve the operators' morale. Problems related to tooling, for example, can be simplified through the use of fixtures common to an entire part family. The economic benefits of the application of group technology become significant when the cost reductions in tool design, production control, materials handling, inventory control, and the like are considered.

All departments in a company can benefit from the introduction of group technology. Parts that are produced in a large number of small batches are most suitable for production in a system organized along these principles. In general, the implementation of group technology will yield advantages in areas such as component standardization, reliability of estimates, effective machine operation, productivity, costing accuracy, customer service, and order potential. At the same time, implementation of group technology can be expected to bring reductions in planning effort, paperwork, setup time, downtime, work in process, work movement, overall production times, finished parts stock, and overall costs.

Production-Oriented Classification and Coding Systems*

Many companies have already implemented group technology, and many more are seriously considering it. Independent surveys made by the University of Michigan and the International Institute of Production Engineering Research (CIRP) have forecast that by about 1990, 70 percent of industry will be using group technology in manufacture.

A scientific parts-coding and classification system is a good adjunct to group technology. Parts-coding systems identify parts with similar geometry or manufacturing processes and help route similar parts to the same manufacturing cell.

* This subsection was written by Dell K. Allen, Professor of Manufacturing Technology, Brigham Young University. It is reprinted with permission from "Technology of Machine Tools," *Machine Tool Task Force Committee Report*, Vol. 2. U.S. Air Force Wright Aeronautical Laboratories; Lawrence Livermore National Laboratories Report No. UCRL-52960, Livermore, CA 94550.

Part families are usually identified either by workpiece classification or by production flow analysis. These classification systems may be broadly grouped into two main categories: (1) design-oriented systems used for workpiece classification, and (2) process-oriented systems used to identify parts which undergo similar processing operations irrespective of their geometry.

Types of Classification Systems

A significant advantage of design-oriented classification systems is that they can be used for retrieval of similar product designs and thus aid in minimizing redundant designs. It has been estimated that it costs nearly $2,000 to introduce each new part in a company product line. It is also known that design redundancy in the United States ranges from 2 to 15 percent. It can readily be seen that design redundancy can become very expensive even in a small plant. Workpiece classification and coding systems can help in reducing unnecessary designs. Prominent design-oriented classification systems include the hierarchical ones developed by Brisch-Bern, Inc., and Lovelace, Lawrence & Co. (Analog system).

Production-oriented classification systems are particularly suited for identifying parts made by similar processes. These systems also identify detailed information relative to types of surfaces to be machined, orientation of features, and other information required for process planning. Examples of production-oriented classification systems are the MDSI CODE, MICLASS, and OPITZ.

These two types of classification systems have been used quite successfully for production-cell design. They are now being called upon to perform new services for which they were not designed, such as computer-assisted process planning, automated time standards, part-family programming, and, potentially, geometric modeling. Recent development efforts by groups such as CAM-I and I-CAM have pointed out some of the shortcomings of design- and process-oriented classification systems when used in these new applications.

There are currently a half-dozen commercial coding systems available. Each of these systems is based upon different perceptions and theories, uses slightly different attributes, and arranges them in different orders.

Stating the Problems

A review of commercially available classification systems reveals that a universal classification system which can be used for all production applications does not exist. Production applications include design retrieval, production cell formation, generative process planning, equipment and tool selection, and automated time standards development. The *general problem* is to develop classification and coding systems which can meet current and future needs in each of these applications.

The *specific problem* is to either tailor existing vendor systems to aid in matching equipment capabilities with workpiece requirements, or to develop in-house systems. Many systems are now being used with some degree of success, and rather than discarding them and starting from scratch, the first approach is to modify existing systems to successfully meet anticipated needs. Modification of existing systems may require a major effort and should not be underestimated. The second approach would be to create a generic system to meet all needs. This is an extremely challenging task, but it is believed that a fairly generic system which can be readily modified to meet changing requirements is possible.

Workpiece Characterization

Workpiece characterization is an essential prerequisite for applying group technology. Workpiece characterization may be accomplished by informal methods or by thorough application of scientific methods of workpiece classifications. In a small shop with a limited number of products, an informal method may be used in which parts are collected and physically grouped into families. In a large shop environment with a variety of products and workpieces, one of the more scientific classification systems is usually required.

State of the Art

There are over 100 different workpiece classification and coding systems in existence. Some of them have been designed for special applications such as forgings, sheet-metal parts, castings, etc., and others for machine parts.

A recent national survey of group technology applications by Ham and Reed (1976) revealed that approximately half of the 50 companies surveyed used no formal workpiece-coding system, 25 percent used commercial systems, and 27 percent used an in-house developed system.

It is commonly accepted that information contained on the part print should be sufficient for production purposes. Three problems arise when this information is interpreted and translated into any classification and coding system. The first problem is that of understanding and interpreting the geometric information and the notes contained on the drawing. The second problem is translating the interpreted information into a prearranged classification system. Occasionally there is not a direct relationship between the attributes included in the classification system and the item being classified. This brings us to the third problem, which is that of interpolation. Here the classifier must either rely on preestablished rules for classifying parts which could be logically placed into either of two or more categories, or he must create his own rules.

Thus, the question arises, what really are the basic items needed for workpiece characterization in a production-oriented classification and coding system? The answer to this question, of course, relates to the intended applications. However, there is some characteristic part drawing information that seems to meet the common needs of many production applications. This information was identified in 1976 by the CAM-I Standards Committee to include workpiece shape or geometry, form features, size, precision, materials, and special treatments, such as for surface finish. To this list should be added quantity of parts and delivery time. These items are discussed briefly below to establish a foundation for matching of workpiece requirements to equipment capability.

Geometry. The geometry of a workpiece includes its gross or basic shape (both external and internal), form features and their relationships, and geometric tolerances. Selected production processes are used to create the basic shape of a workpiece and then to superimpose on that basic shape the various required form features while maintaining the required positional or dimensional tolerances. Primitive shapes from which workpiece geometry is derived include the cylinder, cube, cone, sphere, and the like.

Figure 4-11 shows a composite geometric shape composed of two coaxial cylinders. The two permutations are arrived at by a simple change in the dimensional parameters of length and diameter. It is believed that a set of approximately 150 parametric part families can provide the geometric data base for the vast majority of commercial parts.

The composite part shown may include both positive cylinders and negative cylinders (holes). There is considerable effort being expended to create generalized geometric modeling systems which can be used to create composite parts. These geometric modeling systems are currently very complex and costly, but as advances in computing and graphic systems are made it is expected that these systems will be prevalent.

A low-cost temporary alternative to the above is to utilize the old "tabulated drawing" technique. This technique, greatly enhanced with classification and coding principles, is often now referred to as parametric design.

Form features. Form features are defined as "local geometric characteristics which may be added to a basic shape without changing the family to which it belongs." These features include bevels, holes, slots, joggles, threads, cutouts, and so on. An illustrated glossary of form features has been developed for the CAM-I Process Planning Project. This glossary is intended to promote communication and encourage standardization of form-feature parameters. Figure 4-12, shows examples from the glossary.

Size. The size of a workpiece is an important factor in selecting the basic production process and in matching the workpiece to appropriate equipment. Component parts commonly range in size from tiny watch and instrument parts to large components used on steelmaking, aircraft, and construction equipment. The size range is from less than 1 mm to well over 10,000 mm.

Various coding schemes have been used to divide this broad range of sizes into

Figure 4-11. A composite shape and its permutations.

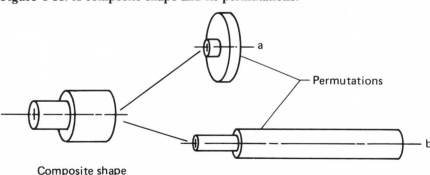

Composite shape

Figure 4-12. Examples of form features from the glossary developed for the CAM-I Process Planning Project.

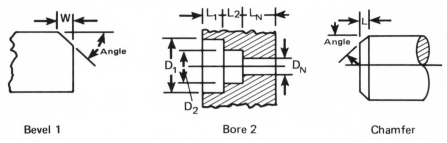

Bevel 1   Bore 2   Chamfer

a few general groupings. Arithmetic, geometric, semilogarithmic, and other schemes have been tried. While little consensus has been reached on which size ranges are preferred, the most useful seem to be those that are related to the type of product being manufactured and to the size of the equipment being used for production.

Precision.   The degree of precision with which a workpiece must be produced has a significant effect on equipment selection, operation routing, inspection requirements, and total production cost. Precision generally includes dimensional, positional, and form accuracy, and surface finish. There is no consensus on the methods for specifying precision or for coding it. This would be a most fruitful area for research.

Material.   The material from which a piece part is produced is important to its proper functioning and to the producibility and cost of the product. While most classification and coding systems include a material code, there is little consensus on either the code symbol or material types. An extensive project has been undertaken at Brigham Young University CAM Laboratory to prepare a hierarchical classification and coding system for all engineering materials. Metals, nonmetals, and composites are included in the classification. A two-character alphanumeric code is used to identify each of the 79 identified material families.

Special treatments.   Special processing treatments are designed to enhance or alter material properties or appearance and to enable the part to better meet its intended functional requirement. Special treatments may be grouped into two broad categories: those for surface finishing (such as painting, electroplating, anodizing, and chromating) and those for modifying material properties (such as hardening and strain-hardening). Relatively few classification systems include special processing treatments although there is ample reason to do so. Here again more research should be undertaken.

Quantity/time requirement.   A most important but often overlooked aspect of classification systems is the quantity/time requirement. Parts needed in quantities of one with a two-day delivery are normally produced in a much different manner from those with quantities of 5,000 and a six-month lead time. This factor can have significant impact on automated process planning.

Manufacturing Process Design

Design for manufacturing should include appropriate applications of value analysis modified by group technology considerations to produce parts and products with the following characteristics.

- Tolerances and specifications optimize the cost/benefit ratio and reduce selective assembly operations.
- Surface-finish requirements are balanced against real need.
- Energy requirements are minimized for changes in configuration.
- Fewer numbers of parts are used to accomplish the product's purpose, to minimize the number of overhead transactions throughout the entire manufacturing process.
- Strategic and scarce materials are conserved.
- Configurations are easy to complete in fewer loadings and handlings, minimizing the setups and the deterioration in geometric relationships and reducing the work-in-process time/inventory.
- Environment in both manufacturing and use is conserved.
- Manufacturing employees or users are not put in physical jeopardy, minimizing liability.
- Utility is for broadest worldwide market.
- Minimum replacement activity is required.
- Competitive positions in the industry are enhanced.

Further integration of the product design and the manufacturing process comes from considering the application of computer-aided design/computer-aided manufacturing (CAD/CAM), which is discussed later in this section. (See "Microprocessors, CAD/CAM, and Robotics.")

Metalworking Processes

Metalworking includes casting, forging, forming, heat treating, welding, cold working, surface treating, finishing, and machining.

Casting

Casting is the production of a desired shape by the introduction of a molten material into a previously prepared cavity or mold and allowing it to solidify. It is one of the oldest methods of producing metal products, particularly intricate pieces. It is almost as easy to make complex shapes as simple ones. Metals most commonly cast are iron, steel, aluminum, brass, magnesium, and zinc alloys. Five common factors are encountered in casting.

■ A mold cavity, allowing for shrinkage of the molten metal as it solidifies, must be produced. The mold material must not be too greatly affected by the flow of molten metal into it, and a suitable melting facility providing an adequate temperature and the means of satisfactory quality production at low cost must be available.

■ A satisfactory method of introducing metal into the mold and assuring the escape of all air or gas must be used; trapped air or gas would cause holes in the casting (porosity).

- Provision for shrinkage without the excessive restraint that causes cracking must be made.
- It must be possible to remove the casting from the mold. There is no problem when sand molds are used, because the sand breaks away from the solidified metal; but serious problems occur with some other types of molds—permanent molds, for example.
- Finishing operations must be performed on castings, which adds to the cost.

Sand casting.   Of the six major types of casting processes, sand casting is the most widely used and accounts for by far the greatest amount of total tonnage of castings produced. Sand casting utilizes sand as a mold material. A new mold must be prepared for each casting. Gravity causes the metal to flow into the mold, and the finished casting varies about $^1/_{16}$ inch in one foot.

To produce a mold, sand is packed around a pattern in the shape of the desired casting. After the sand has been firmly packed, the pattern is removed, leaving a cavity of the desired shape. A sprue hole is cut for the entrance of the metal into the cavity. After the solidification of the casting, the sand mold is broken up so that the casting may be removed.

The design and selection of patterns are vital to the finished quality and cost of the sand casting. The volume determines whether the pattern should be of wood or of metal: High volume requires metal (aluminum, magnesium, or brass); low volume calls for wood (sugar pine or Honduras mahogany). Wood patterns must be protected by coats of shellac. Metal is much more expensive because finishing work and a master pattern are required. Plastics are being used as pattern material because they are cheaper than metal.

Because the shrinkage of different metals varies, each metal requires a special pattern. Cast iron, for example, will shrink $^1/_8$ inch per foot, steel $^1/_4$ inch, aluminum $^5/_{32}$ inch, magnesium $^5/_{32}$ inch, and brass $^3/_{16}$ inch. The pattern maker uses special shrink rules to incorporate the desired shrink allowance in the pattern. Master patterns used to make a metal pattern must have double the shrinkage allowance for the metal that is to be poured into the mold.

Draft is a taper provided on the pattern to allow drawing from the sand. The draft must run to the parting line where the two parts of the pattern come away from each other. Hand drawing requires more draft than machine drawing because the machine will pull directly away from the sand repeatedly, whereas a hand draw needs more allowance for error. The draft is not usually less than 1 degree or $^1/_8$ inch per foot, with a minimum of $^1/_{16}$ inch on any surface. The draft should be kept at a minimum to save excessive machining. A finish allowance must be provided on the casting where machining finishes are required. Usually, $^1/_8$ inch is provided, but the allowance may be more or less, depending on the size and type of casting. Sometimes draft alone may be ample machining stock.

Rap allowance may be considered; the pattern may be rapped to loosen it if there is not ample draft, and in such a case it will need to be made smaller in order to allow for rapping before removing it from the sand.

The types of patterns depend upon the number of duplicate castings to be produced and the complexity of the part. A one-piece or solid pattern is the cheapest and simplest to make but produces the most expensive castings. Loose or split patterns are used to produce moderate quantities and usually have doll pins to ensure the two halves' matching. The upper half of a pattern is called the cope, and the lower half is called the drag. Matched plate patterns are used to produce large quantities. The cope and drag sections are matched on opposite sides of a plate, and the gate and runner system is integral with the plate. Cope and drag patterns are sometimes mounted on separate plates to achieve high production of small or large castings, since two molders can work on the mold. Loose-piece patterns are used when it is impossible to provide draft. Loose pieces can be used on any of the other types of patterns also but, of course, would slow the production of units. A pattern with a follow board to form the parting line is used on loose patterns only.

Generous fillets of $1/4$ inch or $1/8$ inch radius are necessary where sharp corners occur, to prevent shrinkage cracks and stressed intersections. The use of leather or wax for radius filler material is common.

Sometimes metal chaplets need to be used. Their purpose is to cause the thicker sections of the casting to solidify at the same time as the thinner sections. Holes in castings can be cast there by the use of cores. Green sand cores are a part of the mold. Dry sand cores are set in place by the utilization of core prints.

Dry sand cores must possess special properties in order to function properly. They must be of the right hardness; strong enough for handling while green; permeable; collapsible, to prevent cracking and permit easy removal; highly refractory; smooth-surfaced; and constituted to generate a minimum of gas. Core-making equipment includes dump boxes, split core boxes, metal rods for strengthening thin cores, plates for drying flat cores, dryers for drying intricate cores, vents to allow gases to escape, and core-blowing machines in which the sand is blown in. In this case, the box must be vented to allow the trapped air to escape. Cores are baked in batch ovens or continuous ovens, or even with dielectric. They are then finished and assembled. Sometimes they are baked in half and pasted or wired together and scraped so that the parting lines are smooth; then they are daubed with a refractory paste to fill up any irregular surfaces on the core. Some cores are even dipped for a smoother surface, in a graphite, silica, or mica dipping solution.

Shell molding. The shell-molding process is used for better dimensional accuracy and control. In this process, sand and a plastic binder are dumped into a heated pattern so that a $1/8$-inch plastic shell can be cured. The excessive sand is dumped off, and the pattern and shell are placed in the oven for additional curing. The hardened shell is then stripped from the pattern. Two half-shells are clamped or glued together, and the shells are placed in a pouring jacket packed with sand or shot ready for pouring. The metal flows into the mold by gravity, and a new mold must be made for each casting.

The shell process has the advantage of being more accurate because of the use of metal patterns; .003 to .005 inch accuracy can be achieved on small castings. It gives a much smoother casting and is relatively inexpensive equipment for molding, and very complex castings can be made. Low machining costs are the results of the close tolerance casting.

Permanent molding. The necessity of making a new mold for each casting is eliminated through permanent molding. A metal mold is used over and over. Of fine-grain iron or steel, this mold is made in halves and hinged or mounted with a linear motion to open and close. The majority of castings produced from permanent molds are nonferrous, but some are cast iron. Before the molten metal is poured in, the mold is heated to slow the cooling of the molten metal. Usually, a thin refractory coating is placed in the mold. A carbon black coating is added by a torch for cast-iron castings. Dry sand cores can be used.

The advantage of a permanent mold is its low tolerance of $1/64$ inch per foot. The necessary special venting and the ability to produce only simple parts are disadvantages.

A variation of permanent molding is slush casting, in which a shell is allowed to solidify inside the slowly rotating mold and the excess molten metal is poured out. There are variations in the wall section, but this type of casting is suitable for ornaments and similar items that do not need a uniform wall section.

Die casting. This is another variation of permanent molding in that a metallic die is used over and over. Only nonferrous metals are used; the metal is forced into the mold under pressure and held during solidification, resulting in very fine sections and detail. The dies are made of alloy steel with one or more cavities. The die is sometimes made of multiple pieces with complicated cores of steel. The dies are expensive, but the parts are inexpensive in volume runs.

The die-casting cycle consists of closing and locking the die, forcing metal into the die, maintaining the pressure, permitting the metal to solidify, opening the die, and ejecting the casting.

Both gooseneck and cold-chamber machines are used. The gooseneck machines are used for materials of low melting point; the gooseneck is submerged in molten metal. The cold-chamber machines require ladling molten metal for each casting, and higher pressures are used and denser structures gained. Bearings, studs, and the like can be placed in the dies and the metal cast around them.

Aluminum, magnesium, and zinc die castings can be held to plus or minus .003 inch per inch, and .025- to .050-inch wall sections can be cast.

Centrifugal casting. This method utilizes centrifugal force to thrust molten metal against the surface of the mold. The mold is rotated at 300 to 3,000 revolutions per minute while the metal is being poured, creating a uniform, dense metal structure. The mold is metal, but is without cores. A sand lining is normally used for ferrous metals.

Horizontal or vertical pouring is possible. Horizontal pouring creates a cylinder, and vertical pouring creates a paraboloid.

Pipe, brake drums, and similar products are produced by this method.

Investment casting. The investment-casting process is very old, but it became an industrial production process during World War II. Hundreds of years ago, jewelry was the most common example of investment casting: The ring (or whatever the form to be made) was produced in wax; sand was packed around this wax master pattern; and the metal was poured on the wax so that the wax would melt and run out the bottom of the sand mold and the metal would replace the wax cavity. In modern times, the procedure is more complex because of higher volume, lower cost, and high precision parts. A master pattern is first produced and from it a master die. Next, wax patterns or frozen mercury patterns are made and assembled to a common wax sprue. The assembly, called a cluster, is coated with a thin coat of investment material that is a slurry of a finely ground refractory. The final investment is poured around the coated cluster, and the flask is vibrated to remove the entrapped air and settle the investment material around the cluster. The investment is allowed to harden; the wax is melted to run it out of the mold; the mold is preheated to 1,000° to 2,000° F. to help the metal flow; and the metal is poured, cooled, and removed from the mold.

Some of the advantages of investment casting are as follows: very thin sections (as thin as .015 inch); exceptionally smooth surface finish; .005 to .010 inch casting tolerance can be obtained; and only .015 to .040 of machining stock is required. Most investment castings are less than three inches and under two pounds, but much larger parts are possible.

Forging

The strength of metal decreases as temperature increases, with the result that metals are easier to form when hot; thus they require less massive and expensive equipment. The grain structure is also refined and improved by hot working at higher temperatures, in which the grain fiber changes to give greater strength in some parts. And hot working allows a desired shape to be obtained. Forging, the most common method, is the localizing of compressive forces to alter hot metals to the desired shape. Hammering or smith forging is the mechanical hammering of a heated part; the accuracy depends on the operator's skill. Drop forging uses closed impression dies in which the excess metal flows out the parting line and the resulting flash is trimmed off. Drop-forging dies contain multiple cavities which involve the edging, fullering or bending, blocking, and the final shape. Steam hammers or board hammers are used in drop forging; an impact forging machine drives the hammers together, catching the piece between them. The drop-forging dies are made of alloy steel and are expensive. To make a part for drop-forging design, the parting line must be in a single plane and at the center of forging. There must be at least 7 degrees draft on the vertical portions of the die, and generous fillets and radiuses with low and wide ribs are required.

Press forging employs a slow, squeezing action to produce much larger forgings. Less draft is required than for drop-forging. Press forging is a more accurate method than drop forging, and extremely heavy equipment, such as 50,000-ton presses, is used. Upset forging increases the width of bar while decreasing the length; cap screws are an example.

Roll forging is used to draw out sections of bar stock in which semicylindrical rolls are used.

Swaging is hammering metal while it is partially confined. Cylinders can be necked down by this method.

Forming

Rolling. This is a forming process, as are forging, welding, piercing, drawing, extruding, and spinning. It is used for making such products as plates and bars; some are the end products, but most pieces need further processing. Hot rolling is most used and requires very massive and expensive equipment. In this process, two rolls revolve in opposite directions, squeezing between them the metal to be formed. The metal must be uniformly heated for rolling—normally, in a soaking pit in which carbon steel can be heated as high as 2,200° F. It is then finish-rolled at 100° to 200° F. above the critical temperature to prevent cracking.

Continuous mills can run finished plates, bars, and the like, in which each successive roll must turn faster to accommodate the elongation. A speed of 70 miles an hour may be reached at the last roll.

A 3 percent dimensional tolerance in the size of a finished rolled product is normal for hot-rolled products. More or less tolerance is needed, depending upon the type of metal and the size of the piece.

The heating of the metal to make it workable creates the problem of oxidation when it cools. The resultant scale must be removed for some products but is left on as a rust inhibitor for others.

Powder metallurgy. Another means of forming is powder metallurgy; a cold metal powder is pressed into a die and then heated (sintered) at a high temperature. Large quantities of parts can be made economically with this process, and some very difficult pieces can be produced.

Oxide reduction is commonly used to prepare the powders; they are afterward mixed and blended to obtain uniform distribution, coat particles with lubricants, and mix powders of different materials. Water or a solvent may be used to mix better, reduce dusting, and lessen explosion hazards, but powders can be mixed dry. Graphite or stearic acid lubricants reduce die wear and improve flow characteristics.

The powder is pressed by a press of up to 50 tons pressure per square inch. Powder is usually measured into the die by volume but can be weighed to control the quantity of powder, or preformed tablets can be used. Powder flows reluctantly; the compaction of the powder should be uniform over the entire surface to make the pressed part uniformly dense. A double plunger press, which gives a more uniform density, has become the workhorse of the powdered-metal industry.

One hundred pieces per minute can be pressed and ejected from a die mechanically, but the dies wear quickly and are expensive to maintain and replace.

Sintering is done in either a batch-type of continuous oven at 70 to 90 percent of the basic metal's melting temperature to diffuse the powdered particles into a single mass. The time period varies from half an hour to several hours. During the sintering process, volatile materials are driven off, leaving a porous part. The porous openings in the metal can be controlled by introducing volatile materials and impregnating them with lubricant, thus creating a permanently lubricated bearing.

The sintering atmosphere must be controlled to avoid combustion of the powder or oxidation of the part. Partial sintering is sometimes done to give the piece enough strength to be machined before the final sintering. This practice is useful for metals that are hard to machine.

Sizing and finishing are performed on some parts by coining, a method in which the part is placed in a die and hit with a press to press it to size.

On a powdered-iron part which has a 20,000 tensile strength (in pounds per square inch), an additional 12,000 psi can be achieved by coining. Products made by powdered metallurgy are porous bearings and filters, complex gears, carbide which is difficult to machine, motor brushes, and electrical contacts. The bearings are the largest by volume, in which 10 to 40 percent of the volume of the bearing itself is oil.

The advantages of powdered metal are elimination of machining, high production rates, elimination of scrap, production of complex shapes, and wide variations of composition. The disadvantages include low strength, high die cost, high raw materials cost, and design limitations.

Heat Treating

It has long been known that the properties of metals can be changed by heating and cooling the metal. The stability of the metallic properties at various temperatures and rates of cooling can be predicted, and the study of this field has become a science because the physical properties of metals are extremely important to the engineer.

The hardening of steel is the most common form of heat treating. The metal is heated to a high temperature and then rapidly cooled by a quenching material, which may be water, brine, or a hydroxide such as sodium or potassium. The method is to dip the piece into the quench medium or spray the medium on the piece to be quenched. Spraying assures the absence of air pockets, giving a more uniform quench. Oils with a high flash point are used to obtain milder quenches.

Tempering is accomplished after a piece has been hardened. Once the piece is cooled, the hardness is reduced by reheating the part between 400° and 1,200°F and cooling it again in a controlled atmosphere. A wide range of properties is obtainable by the hardening and tempering process, making possible varied products such as spring steel, dies, and tooling. It is important that the engineer understand the properties obtainable by the heating and cooling of metals so that processing can be achieved without changing the properties—or, if desired, so that processing can be achieved to change the properties for the desired product.

Annealing operations are employed to remove stresses, induce softness, or alter toughness, ductility, or other mechanical or electrical properties. The temperature and cooling rate employed are determined by the purpose of the annealing treatment.

The stress-relieve anneal is often employed to remove stresses from welded structures or castings. This is done by heating for several hours at temperatures from 1,000° to 2,000° F., followed by slow cooling.

Surface hardening is achieved by various treatments. In one treatment, carbon is added to the surface so that the steel will be hard on the outside when heated and cooled yet the interior steel piece will still be soft and tough. Another surface-hardening process is nitriding, in which special steels containing aluminum, chromium, molybdenum, or other metals that will form nitrides are used. In still another method, the surface of the metal is heated by electricity or oxyacetylene flame so that only the surface temperature is raised. The work is then quenched rapidly so that the surface is hardened but the core remains soft.

Welding

Metal joining is done by welding, or uniting two pieces of metal into a single piece. Heat and pressure are used together or separately, depending upon the metal properties and end use of the part.

Forge welding is an ancient method in which two pieces are heated and hammered together as the blacksmiths do it. Die welding is useful in the production of pipe manufacture; the flat stock is heated and drawn through a die which forms the pipe and provides pressure on the two butted edges, causing a weld. Cold welding is a process that uses high pressures to bond small parts.

Gas welding came about when oxyacetylene gas was developed to produce a temperature of 6,300° F. This temperature is easily adjustable downward, making it easy to melt thick or thin metals so that they fuse together. Gas welding melts the metals at the point to be joined; pressure is not necessary. Disadvantages of this method are contamination and distortion created by localized heat and flame.

Electric (arc) welding employs an electric arc maintained between the work and an electrode. Alternating or direct current is used. A carbon arc is used for cast iron, copper, and galvanized steel in a process for which the arc is solely a heat source and a filler wire is used when needed to fill a void between the two metals. Metal arc welding uses a metal rod and supplies heat and filler material. The rods, normally, are coated with a flux material.

Inert gas metal arc welding is done by shielding with an inert gas such as helium or argon. Nonconsummable metal electrode welding utilizes the tungsten rod and inert gas shield for welding materials such as magnesium. Atomic hydrogen welding utilizes an alternating current arc between two tungsten electrodes. Hydrogen is fed through the holders so that it is disassociated in the arc, combining with the base metal to give off a high heat. This method is well suited for high-alloy steel welding.

Submerged arc welding maintains an arc beneath a granular flux. The flux is put on just ahead of the copper-coated electrode to give good shielding and, consequently, quality welds achieving up to 30 inches per minute of welding in a one-inch plate.

Inert gas shielded tungsten arc spot welding utilizes inert gases to keep the arc from being consumed.

Thermit welding does not generally employ pressure but a chemical reaction in which the liquid metal supplies the heat and filler. One part aluminum and three parts iron oxide are burned at a temperature above 5,000° F. This method is rarely used, but it may be the only way of welding a very large casting that has been cracked or broken.

Soldering is another form of joining in which coalescence does not take place. Soldering is achieved at below 800° F. The solders are alloys of tin and lead. The higher the percentage of tin, the greater the fluidity. The surfaces must be very clean for soldering; they must be lapped, not butted; and a flux must be used. The greatest strength achieved with solder is 250 pounds per square inch.

In all welding and soldering, fluxes aid the joining by dissolving surface oxides, preventing oxidation during heating, and promoting the flow by lowering the surface tension of molten metal. Residual flux remaining after the use of flux must be removed from the workpiece to prevent corrosion. Cleanliness of the metals before and after welding is essential to good products.

Cold Working

Cold working is the plastic deformation of materials below the recrystallization temperature. Squeezing, bending, and shearing are common cold-working methods; they require expensive equipment but give better accuracy, smoother finish, and better productivity than hot working, and without requiring additional finish. Extrusion, riveting, staking, peening, burnishing, hobbing, coining, and cold heading are all squeezing processes.

Bending is plastic deformation about a linear axis.

Shearing is a method of cutting sheet or plate without burning or chips. Deformation is severely localized, and when 10 to 40 percent of metal thickness is deformed, it exceeds the shear strength. Slitting is a shearing action, as are piercing and blanking. Piercing and blanking also include lancing, perforating, notching, nibbling, chafing, trimming, cutoff, and dinking.

Surface Treating

Cleaning and smoothing methods include abrasive blasting for removing sand or scale; 60 to 100 pounds per square inch of air is used for ferrous metals, and 10 to 60 pounds per square inch for nonferrous. Clean, sharp-edged silica sand or steel grit makes less dust, cleans faster, and rounds the edges considerably.

Tumbling is a means of removing dirt, fins, and other contaminants by placing slug, sand, or sawdust in with the parts and rotating. This is inexpensive, and it may be done wet, which will improve the smoothness of the finished product.

Belt sanding gives a smooth flat surface; wire brushing with a high-speed rotary brush gives another type of finish; barrel rolling is a cutting-down operation using acid, sawdust, or slugs and actually cuts down the part. Buffing is a means of polishing surfaces with a ferrous oxide rouge to improve the sheen. A similar finish is achieved by barrel burnishing, using rounded pins, balls, and the like, rotating them with the parts to peen surfaces.

Vapor degreasing is a method of cleaning by solvent vapor. Alkaline cleaning is used extensively; emulsifiable solvent cleaning is used where alkaline cannot be. Pickling is the use of heated diluted acid to remove oxides only.

Finishing

Painting is done by dipping, spraying, and brushing; adequate ventilation is needed because paint is a fire hazard. Paint is applied in coats of thousandths of an inch thickness per coat. When parts are atomized by air or dipped, a superior finish is achieved. Drying time may be decreased by baking.

Hot dip coatings—galvanizing and tin plating—are other means of finishing, as are phosphate coatings. One such coating is parkerizing, which produces a corrosion-resistant coating .0015 to .0030 inch thick.

Blackening is done to make steel rust-resistant. The part is heated to 1,200° F. for one and one-half hours in a spent carburizing compound and quenched in oil. There are several electrolytic finishes also that add a coating of some nonferrous metal to the surface to improve appearance, reduce corrosion, or inhibit rust.

Machining

Machining operations are usually performed by moving the workpiece against a stationary tool or moving a tool against a stationary workpiece. Some of the standard examples are listed below.

Stationary Workpiece (Moving tools)	Moving Workpiece (Stationary positioned tools)
Boring mills (horizontal and vertical)	Lather (eng., turret, spec.)
Slotters	Planers
Shapers	Milling machines
Gear cutters	Vertical turret lathes
Special mills	Multiple station machines

In purchasing specific modern machine tools, manufacturers should consider tools that reduce machining time, reduce load/unload handling, reduce maintenance, improve quality, enhance flexibility, and reduce cost of operation. With batch and piece manufacturing continuing as production requirements, general-purpose tools are preferred investments, and flexibility is important.

Flexible Manufacturing Systems

There is a general lack of understanding by manufacturers of the total needs for machining in our plants. It is possible to define these needs and create viable systems, ranging from simple to highly sophisticated, for batch and midvolume production.

- The simplest forms are stand-alone computerized numerical control (CNC) machines with ancillary machines or equipment.
- Groups of machine tools can form cells for a production of several parts in a family as determined by, for example, group technology, described previously.
- A flexible manufacturing system (FMS) can be arranged with a group of CNC machines using supervisory computer control, robot assistance, and/or other automated parts handling.
- Multistation rotary index or progress machines with interchangeable heads and/or fixtures can be used for the ultimate in automation.

These increasingly automated processes are directly related to management's ability to use group technology or families of parts and/or optimize use of specific modular parts in the total product line. Consideration of these systems requires a change in manufacturing approach and a reconsideration of organization structures. In planning and getting started, the entire manufacturing organization must begin a "search for sameness" that brings similar requirements for manufacture out from the general morass of differences of parts and processes in most factories. New technology provides a basis for combining machine design, materials handling, and control technology into various manufacturing systems.

Top management should be certain that investigations and studies consider the whole aspect of equipment selection and arrangement in the factory, including the support systems affecting lead time and productivity. Integration into a focused factory situation as discussed under "Planning Flexible Manufacturing Systems" can possibly double present plant output.

Unfortunately, a major portion of the machinery in the United States is not adequately maintained. Total costs and reliability in production schedule attainment are usually overlooked. This condition can be overcome with the addition of preventive maintenance programs (which only a few companies practice with rigor).

Personnel require additional training in maintenance. Much can be accomplished with the use of visual training aids, films, and so forth. Improved maintenance reporting procedures and carefully planned information systems using computers can improve performance immeasurably. Modern technology allows management to develop condition-monitoring systems that include diagnostic software and various types of sensors, vibration analyzers, and so forth. Predictive maintenance is still an infant program, but top-management support can hasten its development. Finally, many plants overload their machinery, and this hastens deterioration and reduces reliability while increasing total costs.

Changes in information systems in the factory are required to support flexible manufacturing systems (FMS). Input data are required in more detail, including technical data for the actual machining process and organizational data that define the location and the time at which particular operations are to take place. Complete discussion and detailed instructions for management in considering FMS are available from the *Machine Tool Task Force Committee Report,* Volume 2 (Lawrence Livermore National Laboratories Report No. UCRL-52960, Livermore, CA 94550) or from machine manufacturers offering assistance in planning these programs, such as Cincinnati-Milacron in Cincinnati, Ohio and Kearney & Trecker in Milwaukee, Wisconsin.

Planning Flexible Manufacturing Systems*

In planning flexible manufacturing systems, the work stations, material flow components, support equipment, and control system have to be designed, on the

* This subsection was written by Dell K. Allen, op. cit.

Figure 4-13. Planning the flexible manufacturing system.

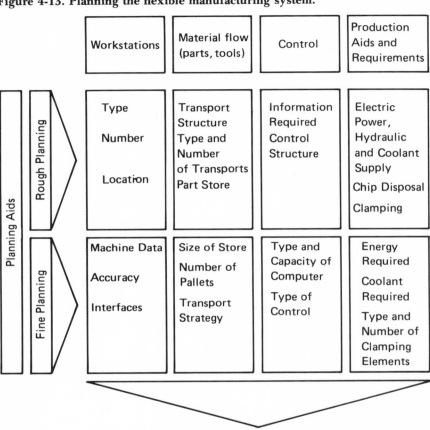

Workstations	Material flow (parts, tools)	Control	Production Aids and Requirements
Type Number Location	Transport Structure Type and Number of Transports Part Store	Information Required Control Structure	Electric Power, Hydraulic and Coolant Supply Chip Disposal Clamping
Machine Data Accuracy Interfaces	Size of Store Number of Pallets Transport Strategy	Type and Capacity of Computer Type of Control	Energy Required Coolant Required Type and Number of Clamping Elements

Layout of the Flexible Manufacturing System

basis of the chosen workpiece spectrum (Figure 4-13). The planning may be divided into overall planning, with the fixing of qualitative data, and detailed planning, with the determination of quantitative values. The planning is an iterative process since there is mutual interaction between the overall and detailed planning.

Above all in planning, the likely behavior of the flexible manufacturing system under operating conditions must be studied. Suitable ways of doing this are by the use of analytical methods, by numerical simulation, and by the application of graph theory.

Integration of the FMS in the Factory

A flexible manufacturing system represents a self-contained production unit within the factory (Figure 4-14). It interfaces with the rest of the factory at the points of its material input and output. Unmachined or premachined parts ready for clamping are fed into the manufacturing system on pallets, and finished— and where possible inspected—parts leave the system in the direction of the assembly department. The equipment for clamping the workpieces at the stations forms part of the flexible manufacturing system. The introduction of the unmachined parts and the removal of the finished parts remain manual operations outside the system.

The flexible manufacturing system also interfaces with the information flow system of the rest of the factory. Data are required concerning the geometry of the parts to be produced as well as about how the machining is to be carried out—that is, machining sequences, speeds, feed rates, and so forth. In addition to this technical information, organizational information concerning capacity loading and work scheduling is also required.

Advantages of FMS

In the manufacturing field, high productivity and automation have been characteristic of most areas of large batch and mass production for many years. In

Figure 4-14. Interfaces of the flexible manufacturing system.

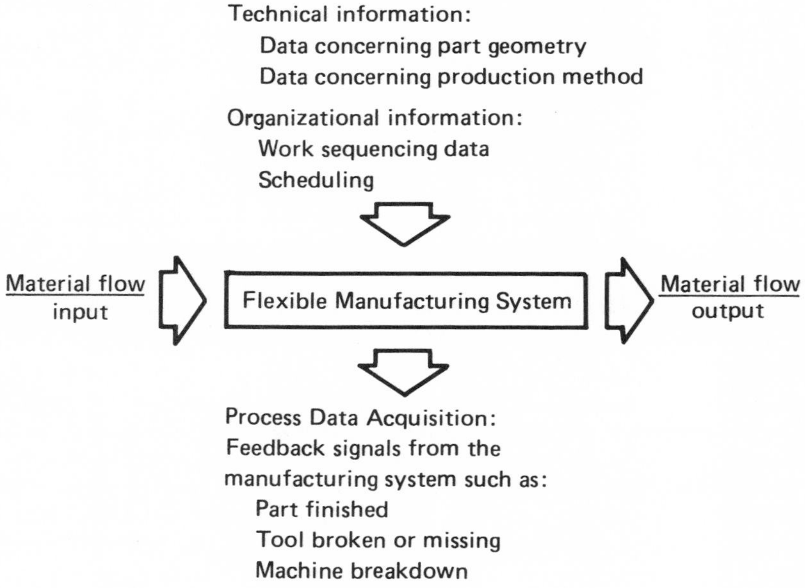

on-off and small batch production, numerical control has brought this general aim a great deal nearer. Whereas with the first NC machines the machining motions alone were automated, the development of the machining center has added the concept of automatic tool changing, thus permitting the automatic machining of complete parts in small batches.

The duties of the operating personnel are reduced to clamping the parts, recharging the tool magazines, putting in the punched tape, and general monitoring of the plant. These functions, however, are so closely connected with the plant itself and its performance that the continual presence of the personnel is necessary. Designs of the machines and equipment take account of such factors as reaction speed of the operating personnel, ease of access, human safety, and so on.

Where the functions mentioned are removed from the plant, the operator no longer has to be present at the scene of the machining; the equipment, in other words, no longer needs to be designed to take account of operator requirements. In the long run, this will certainly lead to considerable changes in the design of machining centers.

Besides breaking the bond, which demanded the physical presence of the operating personnel near the machining operation, the time link has also been loosened: thus, parts may be clamped and unclamped in one shift and the machining may take place in three shifts.

The intensive use of machining centers in the three-shift-per-day system is sufficient on its own to justify the additional part transport and control systems. The loading of expensive machines is also improved by the elimination of organizational shortcomings. The absence of part programs or the presence of errors in existing ones, as well as missing tools, and so forth can be avoided more easily in flexible manufacturing systems than in the normal production situation.

According to Arthur M. Tompson, director of manufacturing engineering at TRW in Cleveland:

> With equipment arranged into manufacturing cells, estimated benefits would be a 40 percent to 70 percent increase in product quality, a 50 percent to 70 percent reduction in machine tools needed, and a 50 percent to 60 percent reduction of work-in-process costs. With flexible manufacturing systems [NC (numerical controlled) machines, robot or pallet load/unload and transport between machines, adaptive control, on-machine sensing, and integrated computer control] we can do even better—all of the above plus the ability to accept a variety of materials, reasonable variations in part configuration (family of parts), and mixed-size lots.

> There is great opportunity for the machine tool industry, the U.S. manufacturing industry, and the nation if the market forces of supplier and customer can be strengthened and the industry managers take a longer-range view of manufacturing trends. This will require something more than lip service if improvement on a national scale is to take place soon. The key to unleashing the wave of technology and productivity is to implement new technology where it pays off, facilitate the flow of private-sector money,

and have industry managers carefully study needs. The world situation is becoming increasingly dynamic, and the timing of new technology introduction is crucial to industrial success in both company and nation.

From a company's standpoint, organizations that can cope with large, rapid changes will succeed. Others will not. From a national standpoint, it is very important that most industrial companies, especially machine tool builders, not only survive but succeed in the world marketplace.

Conclusion and Recommendations

Seventy percent of all manufacturing is performed with batches of less than 50. By 1990, it is predicted that 50 percent of all numerical controlled/direct numerical controlled (NC/DNC) machine tools in operation will be included in systems.

For more than a decade, research-and-development work has been carried out into flexible manufacturing systems. In West Germany, apart from two important pilot plants at the universities of Berlin and Stuttgart, five flexible manufacturing systems are now operating in industry, and this number will increase to 12 in the near future.

Current research work is concentrating on further development of in-process sensors with the aim of reducing the reaction time from the work stations in the case of disturbances as well as improving the acquisition of production status data. Apart from continuing work in the areas of workpiece clamping, transport, and measurement, another key research area is concerned with all aspects of tool management and monitoring in such systems.

Further, because of the high costs relating to the development of DNC software for flexible manufacturing systems, it is important that effort be concentrated on the development of standard modules that can be implemented in new FMS applications with minimal modification using a modular multiprocessor control system.

Tools, Jigs, and Fixtures

Each industry, whether chemical, refining, paper, pottery, or textile, has its own variety of tools for its own kinds of production. Each of these industries will have common tooling used in the maintenance of plant and equipment. Different industries may have basic machine tools—lathes in the metalworking industry, for example. However, the arbors, cutting tools, drill bits, and other parts required by a basic machine tool are the subject of discussion here, rather than the machine tools of productive pieces of equipment.

Classification

Tools are difficult to classify because of their many possible uses. A jig is a tool that clamps the work and guides other tools in performing a cutting operation. A fixture is a tool that holds work while machining operations are being performed on it. General classifications are in use among industries. However, each plant will probably have its own classification system, depending upon its tool storage and control practices. Measuring gauges are often included with the tool categories, or they may be excluded.

Tool Standardization

Tool standardization is increasingly important in consequence of the complexity of industries. Standardization reduces the number of tools stored; it also reduces the clerical and engineering work required to maintain drawings and records of the various tools. As a plant grows, tool standardization becomes more desirable; a plant will support an intensified tool standardization effort at some point in its growth.

A machine tool is a geometrically precise element of the workpiece space. Principal elements of the machine are precise, and tools, jigs, and fixtures affixed to it should be manufactured and developed with no less precision so that the internal geometric relationships and exact distances can be maintained.

All NC machines of all classes—lathes, boring mills, and so on—now use "qualified" tools whose length, mounting surfaces, and other dimensions are plus or minus .0005 inch. Therefore, all setups for manufacture of specific product parts start off close enough to the final position in that complex three-dimensional workpiece space on the machine to permit minor adjustments of up to plus or minus .010 inch to be made by adjusting each of the machine's CNC axis controls.

These expendable cutting tools provide precise cuts that further maintain their geometric position because the actual cutting edges are precisely mounted throwaway carbide wafer tips of the appropriate shape for cutting and chip breaking.

The further need for installing such standardized expendable tool systems comes from the use of tape control for machines that assume predetermined position, shapes, and lengths of these tools to function properly. Most NC machines advance to the final feed rate cutting position at enormous speeds which would cause collision with unexpected shapes, lengths, and so on.

Storage and Control

The location, quantity, and condition of tools are important to efficiency. Planned storage and control of tools can raise efficiency. First, a tool room should be maintained that will control the location and condition of the tools as they are moved from one location to another and as they are used for different operations. Each operation should call for specific tools, and the tool room should be informed before the job so that the tooling will be ready prior to its need on the shop floor. The tool room should hold the workers responsible for all tools allocated to them and used by them. Maintaining tool records of each tool assists in developing historical costs and performance of tools, which will aid in future standardization decisions.

Production Systems

An ideal production system will have the right material at the right place and the right time, and the right number of man-hours and the right number of machine-hours to meet the completion schedule. For an efficient operation it is vital to think through all the detailed steps necessary to achieve this end, and to have a communications network to relay the information to all parties concerned. The degree of success with these two essentials will determine to a large extent the degree of success of the plant. The thinking through is reduced to the communication tools of written factory orders, work-in-progress information, and the end-of-the-line report on completed units produced. The finest plant building with the newest, most modern machine tools may be extremely inefficient if it has no adequate production system. Some very old and antiquated plants are competing with new and modern ones because the antiquated plants do have adequate production systems.

This topic is covered later in this section under the heading "Materials Management." However, the manufacturing planner should note that the production planning function must have a system that generally proceeds in the following sequence. The company must answer these deceptively simple questions:

What are we going to make, build, ship? Plannable product and special product must be described by engineering drawings, data, and bills of materials, and must be maintained by an active and strictly controlled engineering change notice procedure. The engineering change notice procedure must indicate schedules as to when the items or drawings or assemblies on requisition are to appear.

What do we have of what we have to build? An accurate actual inventory record, up to date and complete with allocations or reservations of some materials for specific programs.

What do we have to order? The difference between need and materials on hand requires orders to be placed and properly scheduled, taking into account lead time with economic lot size considerations.

Where is it? A work-in-process reporting system that follows materials so that they can be found any time during the manufacturing process.

What purchase-"finished" records are required to provide materials in usable state? Such records relate to the time-phased manufacturing plan. They report the receipt of materials and indicate that the materials are arriving in accordance with the manufacturing schedules.

Factory work planning and shop floor control are also discussed elsewhere in this Handbook. However, most such systems cannot yet do more to suggest a daily priority or sequence list for the department foreman. Supervisors are required to be abreast of factory product plans so that they can adhere to these final output schedules.

Production control and scheduling techniques have a profound effect on the cost of manufacturing. Programs that are sloppily managed cause extra setup time, the use of revised tooling, and nonstandard, more costly methods. Factory expenses thereby increase.

Even more important, however, is the scheduling plan for the length of time that materials are to be in process. A factory program that assumes a process time of four, five, or six months from start to finish thereby sets the ownership period for that material and thus sets the inventory level and turnover. These inventories require working capital and the direct cost of ownership is associated with having the inventory. Factory management plans that consciously reduce the actual manufacturing time also reduce costs and working capital. Examine policies that set "comfortable" times like one month of raw material plus a month for primary fabrication combined with two more months of machining plus assembly time. Such planning is convenient and easier on the managers but it is more costly and requires higher investment.

Utliization Studies

Overall plant layout, including machine utilization records (taking into account peak periods), storage facilities, individual work areas, materials handling, and materials flow, is carefully analyzed to determine whether present plant and equipment are properly utilized or whether a new layout would increase capacity and efficiency. After the study has been completed, a managerial decision is made to determine whether to plan requirements for present sales volume (including seasonal peaks) or for expected sales volume. If requirements for future volume are to be planned, the period of time (one, two, five, or ten years) and expected sale levels at that time are projected. Next, an economic decision is made as to whether it would be less expensive to utilize present plant and equipment better (by redesigning the plant layout, by transferring operations from one machine to another, or by adding a second or third shift), or whether the company should subcontract or add additional space and buy additional equipment. By this type of careful evaluation of alternatives, present plant and equipment utilization as well as future needs can be determined systematically.

Individual Operational Analysis

Individual operational analysis is the systematic reduction of each of the methods used to produce an item into its simplest component parts. Every facet of the individual job, including all the tools, fixtures, equipment, tolerances, work layout, and waste, is carefully examined. The reasonableness and necessity of every detail of each individual job is questioned; nothing is accepted without careful examination. Next, every necessary facet of the operation is further broken down into its simplest parts with the intent of further elimination, simplification, and study. Individual operational analysis charts are frequently used on complex jobs to make certain that every detail is questioned and investigated. Depending upon the complexity of the operation and the potential savings, these chart checklists can be either formally filled in or informally used as a guide.

Work Methods Analysis

Methods analysis is one of the main tools used in reducing labor costs. To use it effectively, it is necessary to analyze procedures, operations, and systems; establish standards of accomplishment; and control performance. Methods analysis involves the systematic study of each job with the intent of eliminating unnecessary operations; standardizing equipment, tools, methods, and working conditions; and measuring the time required to perform each operation.

To determine which analytical tool to use, a comparison is made between the anticipated return and the costs involved in applying the various techniques. Depending upon an evaluation of costs versus savings, process charts, man/machine charts, operation charts, or other techniques may be indicated.

Standardization. In order to control performance, it is important to establish an accurate measurement of the time required to perform each job; this necessitates the standardization of equipment, production material, tools, and fixtures. Methods also should be standardized in all parts of the plant. This will help assure that labor standards will be uniformly and fairly established, thereby reducing grievances and facilitating the rapid introduction of improvements in all areas of the plant with a minimum of time and effort.

Labor standards. To effectively control manufacturing labor costs and obtain a fair day's work from employee's, labor standards must be established throughout the company. To assure accuracy (which will help reduce labor problems), labor standards are normally established on the basis of work measurement. Standards are best established by an individual trained in work measurement techniques who is not directly responsible for the jobs being studied. These labor standards can then be effectively enforced, controlled, and used as a basis for manpower planning and wage incentives.

Computer Applications

Many different industries have begun to use the computer to achieve cost savings. The computer has made notable contributions to profitability in job shops through the effective use of numerically controlled machines. In assembly shop operations, the computer has reduced overall costs by relating and controlling customer orders, inventory, and production scheduling. Moreover, the process industry has profited by using the computer for optimum blending, which results in fewer errors and more consistent quality. Additional opportunities for cost savings by the use of a computer include the reduction of distribution costs, maintenance costs, scrap costs, and inventory carrying costs.

Predetermined work standards providing a uniform base or relationship between occupations and tasks are available as motion time measurement (MTM) and time management units (TMU). Manuals, descriptions, and consultation are available for their effective application.

□ *C. Eugene Moore (and Robert E. McCoy and John J. McCrea,
the original authors of this now substantially revised section)*

MICROPROCESSORS, CAD/CAM, AND ROBOTICS

The integration of telecommunications, the microprocessor, automation, and robotics is revolutionizing the manufacturing process. This revolution permits the "real time" management of the manufacturing cycle, reducing downtime, inventory, and through-put time, improving machine utilization, monitoring quality, and at the same time providing a constant stream of data on the cost of the product.

An example implemented in various phases and to varying degrees will help illustrate what goes on.

Materials are ordered automatically on the basis of a computer's evaluation of the stock status, and purchase orders are transmitted to suppliers. As materials are received, the computer balances the inventory and allocates parts to the various jobs in progress. The cost deck is upgraded to the latest price for the parts received. Parts being manufactured are run by tape or other preprogrammed instructions that were prepared at the time "drawings" were generated. Machine utilization is noted and lines are automatically "balanced." Costs are accumulated continuously and efficiency is monitored constantly.

Robots move parts from one machinery center to another and perform assembly operations at "assembly centers." The factory lights are dim, and the temperature of the facility is reduced to the comfort level of the *machines*. The final product is packaged by robots, and shipping labels are generated from preprogrammed instructions. Operators in the plant monitor consoles as a system and zero in on specific operations as required. The industrial manager can "read" an hourly or daily profit and loss statement. All these things are possible with the technology and hardware that exist today. The need to reduce costs and increase productivity will be the engine that will drive this revolution.

*Economic Incentives**

Manufacturing normally contributes approximately 30 percent of the gross national product of modern industrialized countries. Yet in spite of that, and although manufacturing is normally thought of as a highly productive and efficient activity, it is not generally so. For example, this is clearly true of batch-type metalworking manufacturing, which normally accounts for about 40 percent of total manufacturing employment. Mass-production manufacturing systems such as automotive transfer lines account for less than 25 percent of metalworking parts manufacture. In fact, 75 percent of such parts are manufactured in lots consisting of fewer than 50 pieces.

It has been shown that when the life of the average workpiece in batch-type metal-cutting production shops is analyzed, only about 5 percent of its time is actually spent on machine tools, and of that 5 percent, only about 30 percent (or 1.5 percent of the overall time) is actually spent as productive time in removing metal. This situation can hardly be called economical or productive. Further, it truly pinpoints the two main areas where the greatest improvement in the economy and productivity of metalworking can be made today.

The first of these areas of potential improvement is reduction of time of parts in process in the shop. This in turn would reduce the extremely high inventories of unfinished parts on the shop floor and of finished parts waiting for others in process so that assembly of the product can proceed. These inventories could potentially be reduced by up to 90 percent, thereby greatly decreasing indirect capital and labor costs and improving productivity.

Here, indeed, is a major incentive to development and implementation of the computer-integrated automatic factory.

The second area of potentially great improvement is in increasing machine uti-

---

* This subsection is based on material by M. Eugene Merchant, "Future Trends in Manufacturing Toward the Year 2000," CIRP *Annals*, Vol, 25, No. 2 (1976), pp. 473–476.

lization time. The average machine spends approximately 50 percent of its time waiting for parts to work on because of the 95 percent time in transit. As a result, the average machine tool in a batch-type shop is being used productively (that is, actually cutting metal) only about 15 percent of the time. Thus potentially machine use could be increased by 600 percent or more. The resulting reduction in direct labor and overhead costs and increase in productivity could be enormous.

Another major economic consideration today is the rapidly rising cost of manufacturing labor (compensation per man-hour) relative to manufacturing productivity (output per man-hour). This situation can be reversed only by improving the rate of increase of manufacturing productivity, decreasing the degree of labor intensiveness of manufacturing, or both. Both these aims can be accomplished by development and implementation of the computer-integrated automatic factory, and therefore this possibility offers an additional major incentive to advancement of such technology.

Social Incentives

Today, major social forces are also emerging which provide strong incentives for early implementation of the computer-integrated automatic factory. Among these trends, three sets of changing attitudes toward manufacturing are particularly significant: those of workers, those of employers, and those of government.

Concerning the first of these, there is a steadily increasing reluctance of workers to continue to expose themselves to the manufacturing environment. As a result, there is a shortage of manufacturing workers in all major industrialized countries of the world. As for employers, they are now clearly recognizing the human need for the nature of work to be such that the worker can not only be assured of safe and healthy conditions but can gain satisfaction in performing it. Finally, the third significant trend in attitudes toward manufacturing is the recognition by governments throughout the world that workers should be freed from unsafe or unhealthful working conditions.

The economic need plus the political and sociological forces in place will propel this manufacturing revolution through the remainder of the twentieth century and into the twenty-first.

What follows is a brief description of the technological work that has been and is taking place to make this possible. We shall discuss the electronics revolution — the microprocessor; CAD (computer-aided design), CAM (computer-aided manufacturing), and numerical control; as well as robotics. Although realization of the fully computer integrated automatic factory is the goal, this will be an evolutionary process.

Microprocessors*

The transistor was invented in the 1940s. At the time, it was not recognized as one of the most significant advances of technology. In fact, the real value of this new device was not universally accepted until the 1950s and early 1960s. Because

* This subsection is based on C. L. Lynes, *Microprocessors and Change,* Society of Manufacturing Engineers Technical Paper EE 77–856 (1977).

of this device, what was previously built from huge power-hungry vacuum tubes could be put into a small fraction of the space and use very small amounts of power. Moreover, the application for electronics was expanded into areas never before envisioned, such as the space program, which could never have been developed without this semiconductor technology. Portable television sets, radios, tape recorders, and stereo sets all have their foundations in this technology.

In the 1960s there was another huge advance when it was found that many of these little transistors could be put on the same crystal structure to create whole circuit functions. This is what today is called a monolithic integrated circuit. In the digital electronics world, these functions were called gates, flip-flops, registers, counters, and so forth. These first circuits became known as small-scale integration (SSI). The various families were resistor-transistor logic (RTL), diode-transistor logic (DTL), and transistor-transistor logic (TTL). These various ways of connecting transistors inside an integrated circuit package have become the industry standards.

As the microcircuit technology advanced to more complex functions in the late 1960s and the early 1970s, medium-scale integration (MSI) circuits were developed. During the past decade, advances have been made in extremely complex large-scale integration (LSI) circuits, which typify the level of complexity of today's microprocessor.

An example will serve to illustrate these developments over the last 30 years. In 1946 the first digital computer was constructed from 16,000 vacuum tubes for logic elements, 7,000 relays and switches for memory, 70,000 resistors, and 20,000 capacitors. This computer, called Eniac, occupied 200 cubic feet of space, weighed 30 tons, consumed 140,000 watts of power, and operated at speeds only up to 100 KHz. To fill the same space as Eniac would require 30 million of the new Fairchild F3870 single-chip microprocessor, which has about the same computing power as Eniac but is housed in a single 40-pin dual-in-line package. This microprocessor device weighs about an ounce, consumes only one-third of a watt, and runs at 2 MHz. The phrase "little, but mighty" has never had greater meaning. In 1946, Eniac cost many millions of dollars. In contrast, the F3870, even at today's inflated price, costs less than $10.00 when 100 or more are purchased.

The evolution of the microprocessor began in 1971 when a company in San Antonio called Datapoint contracted with a new West Coast semiconductor company called Intel to develop a custom-programmed logic device for use in Datapoint processing equipment. Although this custom device (the Intel 4004) turned out to be too slow for the application at Datapoint, it proved to be satisfactory for many other applications. Improvements have been made over the years, and every major manufacturer of semiconductors now has one or more microprocessor chips. The most popular are Fairchild's F-8 family, Intel's 8080, Motorola's 6800, Zilog's X-80, and Texas Instruments' TMS9900. These are compared in Figure 4-15, which rates each one on a performance versus price graph.

Applications

There are two distinct marketplaces for the microprocessors. In the first, the minicomputer-like systems that are wanted are characterized by high perform-

Figure 4-15. Comparison of popular microprocessors.

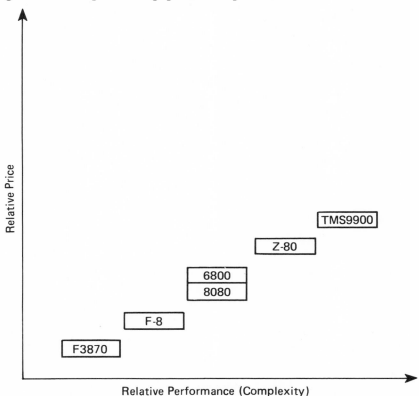

ance, lots of memory, components cost of over $100.00, and availability of high-level software languages; in addition, they are used in relatively low volume. The software for this type of application tends to be modular, easily modified, and heavily documented. Important features of such systems are speed, computing power, interrupt handling, subroutine nesting, direct memory access (DMA), and ready software support from the manufacturer of the development system. The most popular microprocessors that fit this category are the Intel 8080 and the Motorola 6800.

In the other market segment, the controller market, the key feature is cost not performance. The microprocessor wanted here is characterized by less perform-ance, minimum memory, few overall parts that cost substantially less than $100.00, and little need for high-level languages and their associated inefficien-cies; and it is used in large volume. The software for this type of application is optimized to use the least amount of required memory, and once the software is completed there is no need to maintain or support it. Documentation is usually not available to the final user, who has little use for it. In fact, in some applications, such as video games, the software is a very closely guarded secret. The single most important feature of such a system is to control some device or process with the least number of parts, at the highest reliability, and at the lowest possible cost, and the microprocessor provides these features better than costly mechanical relays and switches. The most widely used microprocessor for this type of application is the Fairchild F-8.

Essentially, microprocessors are used because (1) they simplify the designer's job by integrating complex functions on a single circuit; (2) they add flexibility in that the same basic design can be used for several related functions with changes only in software; (3) they simplify the manufacturing process by reducing the required number of circuit parts; (4) they reduce cost by replacing many complex circuits with a few relatively low-cost devices; and (5) they allow new functions and applications which were heretofore too costly to implement. The real value of this technology is just being realized, both for today's applications and for future applications.

The kinds of applications one sees today for the microprocessor are staggering. In any city of 50,000 population or more there is almost certainly a store where any citizen who desires can purchase, for a few hundred dollars, more computer than was available at any price 20 years ago. This is the hobbyist market. A dentist or doctor who wants to keep accounting records on computer can now afford to purchase and maintain a custom computer at a fraction of the rental cost of time on a large IBM which is a standard canned format determined by IBM. Video games, most of which are microprocessor-controlled, are now available in all shapes and sizes. Some games now come with cartridges, so that changing games is easy and cheap. Microprocessors now control TV tuning, auto ignition, microwave ovens, all kinds of kitchen appliances, oil pipelines, telephone communication, radio transmission, CB radios, and even children's toys. They have invaded everyday life to such an extent that within five years they will be indispensable. This proliferation will open up tremendous opportunities for a new breed of technical engineer.

New Breed of Engineer

Engineers of today are so specialized that few have a working knowledge of any discipline other than their own. They begin to specialize sometime during their college education, and after graduation they go to work for some company that will further specialize their talents. They work as mechanical engineers who design mechanical chassis to house electronics, or as electrical engineers who design transformers for 60-cycle AC power distribution. With the onset of computer technology came a whole new profession called computer programming, and the average member of this profession cares little how the actual hardware of the computer works. He is used to dealing with high-level language and has needed no intimate knowledge of gates and latches. Engineers, on the other hand, know the internal hardware but have little knowledge of software. This segmentation of software and hardware will be untenable in the future and can be already seen weakening in the microprocessor world. It is from this microprocessor technology that the new engineer will emerge.

This new engineer could be called a general engineer because he will have general knowledge rather than specialized knowledge. He will be conversant in as broad a spectrum of technology as he is capable of handling, but not to any real depth. He will have to take a systems approach to a design problem and use his broad knowledge to discern which technologies can be brought to bear. It will be his job to determine if a design is feasible, to develop functional specification, and, when this task is complete, to turn it over to the specialists for the detail design. The following example illustrates the value of such an engineer.

Let us suppose that the engineer must design a system to automatically control a remote high-power radio transmitter that is many miles from the studio. To design such a system requires a working knowledge of digital design, analog design, instrumentation, RF communication design, telephone network design (if the transmitter is controlled via telephone lines), computer programming, and the ability to relate all these different areas to create a homogeneous design. The general engineer determines the feasibility and overall system elements needed. He will write a functional specification delineating the overall equipment and features required, and upon completion of this document he will turn over the detail design of each system element to specialists: computer design to digital engineers; circuit design to electrical engineers; RF design to radio engineers; etc. An efficient and cost-effective design will thus be completed in the minimum time. This type of engineer will, with his broad view, also develop as yet unknown and not necessarily obvious products and services for the future.

Types of Microprocessors*

To determine the type of microprocessor required, several factors must be considered following an exact definition of the task. Among the more significant factors are speed of response (from input stimulus to output response); task complexity; costs, including development and running; test and repair; and product improvements.

In addition to the factors to be considered in the design approach, there are a number of approaches to choose from. Here we shall consider discrete logic (relay or semiconductor), the single-bit logic processor, and the metal-oxide semiconductor (MOS) parallel microprocessor. Each of these logic implementations could be useful in overlapping applications. The attempt here will be to show the major strengths and weaknesses of each approach as it applies to manufacturing and automation applications.

Discrete logic. When a particular task is easily defined as a logical relationship between input and output, then a collection of gates or relays may be appropriate. The various counters, latches, and so forth that are available with semiconductor technology enhance its flexibility over relay logic. Familiarity with relays,

---

* This subsection is based on Mitch Gooze, *Capabilities and Cost: Effectiveness of Microprocessors in Manufacturing and Automation Applications,* Society of Manufacturing Engineers Technical Paper EE 77–918 (1977).

however, will often cause a plant engineer to bypass discrete semiconductor logic. In either case, as the task becomes more complex and the output becomes less directly related to the input as a pure logic function, discrete logic implementation will become more costly. This cost increase is due to the additional design time and additional hardware required. The additional hardware also increases repair and maintenance costs. Lastly, since the logic implementation was optimized for the particular task defined, any change in that task could require a complete system redesign.

Single-bit microprocessors. In an attempt to solve some of the problems encountered with the discrete logic approach, a similar device was introduced, designed to operate on inputs and outputs one at a time and configured to resemble a relay system. These devices became known to the controls industry as programmable logic controllers (PLCs). The central architecture of a PLC has now been developed as an integrated circuit, the Motorola MC145008 industrial control unit (ICU).

To perform functions similar to a set of gates, a minimal number of instructions are required (the 14500 has 16 instructions). Instructions are performed serially to give a particular output. As with other programmable computers, once a particular logic relationship has been defined, it can be repeated as often as necessary by using loops and subroutines.

The single-bit processor has the usual advantages of any processor in that a particular task can be readily modified by changing software. The ICU also has the advantage of speed over the MOS parallel processor for bit decisions, but it lacks the math capability found in most MOS processors.

MOS parallel microprocessors. MOS (metal-oxide semiconductor) microprocessors form the bulk of interest in controllers today. Part of the reason is that they have been around now for several years, but more important is their adaptability to a wide range of applications and their cost-effectiveness in these applications. Since, with each passing year, the capabilities of these processors are increasing while their costs continue to decrease, their usage should continue to increase.

CAD/CAM and Numerical Control

The United States Air Force Program for Integrated Computer Aided Manufacturing (ICAM) was brought about by the Air Force need to improve manufacturing productivity in the aerospace industry. ICAM is essentially a program and development plan to produce systematically reliable computer-based modules for efficient manufacturing operations. This is a long-range effort with many private-sector participants. The basis of the program is to establish a logic path for manufacturing operations; to define the information, processes, tools, and flow of material as well as materials-handling systems; and to integrate them into a whole. The important thing is that it is being developed with existing technology and hardware.

In recent years, computer graphics have grown explosively. For example, designs of structural members for aircraft and automobiles are now drawn by the use of computer graphic techniques. A mechanical member is defined by means of conventional three-dimensional coordinates. On the basis of this definition, stress analyses are performed to determine the load-bearing properties. In turn, drawings and tapes for profile milling machines are generated.

The garment industry is also using computer graphics: After a style is developed, various sizes are generated by the computer. The optimization of the cutting from the bolt of cloth is accomplished through the computer.

Numerical control—that is, performing operations from preprogrammed instructions—has been around for 20 years. These preprogrammed instructions, usually prepared on perforated tapes, are rapidly being replaced by the microcomputers. It is expected that few if any machine or control builders will offer another type of numerical control.

Numerical control in the broad sense of the term—control by coded instructions with no implications of tape, hardware, software, etc.—is expected to become *the* way to do any job in the manufacturing process. According to James L. Koontz, Ex-Cell-O Corporation group vice president for machine tools, "as the floor-mounted control shrinks and disappears into the machine, and as hydraulics give way to all-electric drives, tomorrow's machines will become simpler, more compact, and be thought of as just conventional machines." Four- and five-axis contouring machines will become the standard machines of tomorrow, and hardly anything except numerically controlled machines will even be considered for use in manufacturing.

Another trend that will affect machine controls is the move away from centralized processing. According to National Semiconductor Corporation, low-priced microprocessors will catalyze tremendous growth in multiprocessor distributed-intelligence systems. Distributed processing using microprocessors will be the wave of the future, according to the experts, and the world of machine controls will benefit from the spinoffs as distributed processing technology continues to mature.

"CAD is the application of computers to design where the designer converses directly with the computer by using a graphic or nongraphic console in such a manner that the problem-solving processes are highly responsive and essentially uninterrupted," according to *Production Engineering* (April 1977).

The proper emphasis is in computer-aided design and computer-aided manufacturing. For the purposes of this discussion, CAD/CAM is not a turnkey graphic computer system, a software program or aggregate or system of programs, or a department or group so named. According to Kenneth C. Bonine, data systems specialist at General Dynamics Corporation, CAD/CAM *is* the integration of the following five elements into the process for specifying, designing, fabricating, and testing a product:

1. *A philosophy* of using the computer to do the computational and rote parts, assisting the person who is the creative, innovative partner in the process in a responsive, on-line fashion.
2. The *people* who are the key resource to be optimized. They are the ones who *create* the designs, devise and implement the manufacturing processes, and make the key decisions.
3. The *procedures* which define the organized and necessary flow and verifi-

cation of data. They also delineate the way in which control is effected and the appropriate decision-making organization.

4. The *programs*—The software (system utility routines, specific application programs) that is used to effect the analysis, geometry definition, tool path, etc.
5. The *processors*—The computers, peripherals (terminals, printers, plotters, etc.) and communications equipment needed to interconnect them to each other and to any machine tool or other device used in the total process of creating, building, and testing a product.*

Basics of Robotics†

Industrial robots exist in a wide range of capabilities and configurations. However, they commonly consist of several similar major components: the manipulator, the controller, and the power supply. These components are described in basic terms. The most common robot configurations are related to the coordinate systems in which they function: cylindrical, spherical, or jointed-spherical. Significant features and common characteristics of nonservo and servo-controlled robots are explored in depth. Interfacing of robots and associated equipment for coordinated interaction is described. Some future trends in robot development are discussed.

General Characteristics

Industrial robots are available in a wide range of capabilities and configurations. Basically, however, they consist of several major components: the manipulator or "mechanical unit" which actually performs the manipulative functions, the controller or "brain" which stores data and directs the movement of the manipulator, and the power supply which provides energy to the manipulator.

The manipulator is a series of mechanical linkages and joints capable of movement in various directions to perform the work of the robot. These mechanisms are driven by actuators which may be pneumatic or hydraulic cylinders, hydraulic rotary actuators, or electric motors. The actuators may be coupled directly to the mechanical links or joints or may drive indirectly through gears, chains, or ball screws. In the case of pneumatic or hydraulic drives, the flow of air or oil to the actuators is controlled by valves mounted on the manipulator.

Feedback devices are installed to sense the positions of the various links and joints and transmit this information to the controller. These feedback devices may be simply limit switches actuated by the robot's arm or position-measuring devices such as encoders, potentiometers or resolvers, and/or tachometers to measure speed. Depending on the devices used, the feedback data are either digital or analog.

* *Economic Considerations of CAD/CAM*, Society of Manufacturing Engineers, 81–952 (1981).
† This section is reprinted from William J. Tanner, "Basics of Robotics," *Industrial Robots* (Vol. 1), Society of Manufacturing Engineers, MS 77–734 (1977).

The controller has a threefold function: first, to initiate and terminate motions of the manipulator in a desired sequence and at desired points; second, to store, position, and sequence data in memory; and third, to interface with the "outside world."

Robot controllers run the gamut from simple step sequencers through pneumatic logic systems, diode matrix boards, electronic sequencers, and microprocessors to minicomputers. The controller may either be an integral part of the manipulator or housed in a separate cabinet.

The complexity of the controller both determines and is determined by the capabilities of the robot. Simple nonservo devices usually employ some form of step sequencer. Servo-controlled robots use a combination of sequencer and data storage (memory). This may be as simple as an electronic counter, patch board, or diode matrix and series of potentiometers or as sophisticated as a minicomputer with core memory. Other memory devices employed include magnetic tape, magnetic disc, plated wire, and semiconductor (solid state RAM). Processor or computer-based controller operating systems may be hard wired, stored in core memory, or programmed in ROM (read only memory).

The controller initiates and terminates the motions of the manipulator through interfaces with the manipulator's control valves and feedback devices and may also perform complex arithmetic functions to control path, speed, and position. Another interface with the outside world provides two-way communications between the controller and ancillary devices. This interface allows the manipulator to interact with whatever other equipment is associated with the robot's task.

The function of the power supply is to provide energy to the manipulator's actuators. In the case of electrically driven robots, the power supply functions basically to regulate the incoming electrical energy. Power for pneumatically actuated robots is usually supplied by a remote compressor which may also service other equipment.

Hydraulically actuated robots normally include a hydraulic power supply as either an integral part of the manipulator or as a separate unit. The hydraulic system generally follows straightforward industrial practice and consists of an electric motor-driven pump, filter, reservoir, and, usually, a heat exchanger (either air or water). These robots normally operate on petroleum-based hydraulic fluid; however, most are available with special seals for operation on fire-retardant fluid.

Mechanical arrangements of the manipulator are widely varied among the robots available today, as is the terminology used to describe these mechanical components and motions. The most common configurations are best described in relation to their coordinate systems: cylindrical, spherical, and jointed-spherical.

The cylindrical coordinate robots include the Pacer, Versatran, and Auto-Place. Their configuration consists of a horizontal arm mounted on a vertical column, which, in turn, is mounted on a rotating base. The horizontal arm moves in and out; its carriage moves up and down on a vertical column and these two members rotate as a unit on the base. Thus, the working area or envelope is a portion of a cylinder.

The Unimate and Prab are typical of robots having a spherical coordinate system. Their configuration is similar to the turret of a tank. An arm moves in and out, pivots in a vertical plane, and rotates in a horizontal plane about the base. The work envelope is a portion of a sphere.

The third coordinate system, jointed-spherical or jointed-arm, is used by the ASEA and Cincinnati Milacron robots. This configuration consists of a base or trunk and an upper arm and forearm which move in a vertical plane through the trunk. An "elbow" joint is located between the forearm and upper arm and a "shoulder" joint is located between the upper arm and the trunk. Rotary motion in a horizontal plane is also provided at the shoulder joint. The work envelope approximates a portion of a sphere.

These members comprise the major axes or "degrees of freedom" of the robot. As many as three additional degrees of freedom are provided at the extremity of the robot arm in a unit commonly called a "wrist." Wrist axes include "roll" (rotation in a plane perpendicular to the end of the arm), "pitch" (rotation in a vertical plane through of the arm), and "yaw" (rotation in a horizontal plane through the arm).

Additional motions may be provided by mounting the robot on a two-axis (X-Y) table or on a track on the floor or overhead. Many of the robots available are "modular" in design. That is, the user may select as few as two or as many as seven or eight degrees of freedom, depending upon his needs.

A mounting surface is provided on the last axis of the wrist for installation of the tool or gripper with which the robot performs its intended task. These devices are usually unique to the robot application and are thus provided by the user. However, several robot manufacturers offer a selection of devices for grasping parts which may be directly applicable or adaptable to the particular task to be performed.

Classification

Robots may be generally classified as nonservo or servo-controlled devices. For purposes of discussion, this is convenient, since each classification has uniquely common characteristics. The servo-controlled class can be further separated into point-to-point and continuous path devices, each with unique characteristics and applications.

Nonservo robots. Nonservo robots are often referred to as "end point," "pick and place," "bang-bang," or "limited sequence" robots. However, these terms imply limited capability and restricted applicability, which is not necessarily the case. The term "nonservo" is more descriptive and less restrictive than the others used.

A typical operating sequence of a hydraulic or pneumatic nonservo robot is as follows:

- Upon start of program execution, the sequencer/controller initiates signals to control valves on the manipulator's actuators.
- The valves open, admitting air or oil to the actuators and the members begin to move.

□ The valves remain open and the members continue to move until physically restrained by contact with end stops.

□ Limit switches signal the end of travel to the controller, which then commands the control valves to close.

□ The sequencer then indexes to the next step and the controller again outputs signals. These may again be to the control valves on the actuators or to an external device such as a gripper.

□ The process is repeated until the entire sequence of steps has been executed.

The significant features of a nonservo robot are:

□ The manipulator's various members move until the limits of travel (end stops) are reached. Thus there are usually only two positions for each axis to assume.

□ The sequencer provides the capability for many motions in a program, but only to the end points of each axis.

□ Deceleration at the approach to the stops may be provided by valving or shock absorbers.

□ It is feasible to activate intermediate stops on some axes to provide more than two positions; however, there is a practical limit to the number of such stops which can be installed.

□ Although this mode of operation is commonly used on the smaller robots, it is applicable to larger units also.

□ The programmed sequence can be conditionally modified through appropriate external sensors; however, this class of robots usually is restricted to the performance of single programs.

□ Programming is done by setting up the desired sequence of moves and by adjusting the end stops for each axis.

Common characteristics of nonservo robots include:

□ Relatively high speed is possible, owing to the generally smaller size of the manipulator and full flow of air or oil through the control valves.

□ Repeatability to within 0.25 mm (0.010 in.) is attainable on the smaller units.

□ These robots are relatively low in cost; simple to operate, program, and maintain; and highly reliable.

□ These robots have limited flexibility in terms of program capacity and positioning capability.

Typical nonservo robots manufactured or marketed in the United States include Auto-Place, Kelate, PickOmatic, and Prab.

Servo-controlled robots. The second major class of robots are servo-controlled. The typical operating sequence of a servo-controlled robot is as follows:

□ Upon start of program execution, the controller addresses the memory location of the first command position and also reads the actual position of the various axes as measured by the position feedback system.

□ These two sets of data are compared and their differences, commonly called "error signals," are amplified and transmitted as "command signals" to servo valves for the actuator of each axis.

□ The servo valves, operating at constant pressure, control flow to the manipulator's actuators, the flow being proportional to the electrical current level of the command signals.

□ As the actuators move the manipulator's axes, feedback devices such as encoders, potentiometers, resolvers, and tachometers send position (and, in some cases, velocity) data back to the controller. These "feedback signals" are compared with the desired position data and new error signals are generated, amplified, and sent as command signals to the servo valves.

□ This process continues until the error signals are effectively reduced to zero, whereupon the servo valves reach null, flow to the actuators is blocked, and the axes come to rest at the desired position.

□ The controller then addresses the next memory location and responds appropriately to the data stored there. This may be another positioning sequence for the manipulator or a signal to an external device.The process is repeated sequentially until the entire set of data, or "program," has been executed.

The significant features of a servo-controlled robot are:

□ The manipulator's various members can be commanded to move and stop anywhere within their limits of travel, rather than only at the extremes.

□ Since the servo valves modulate flow, it is feasible to control the velocity, acceleration, and deceleration of the various axes as they move between programmed points.

□ Generally, the memory capacity is large enough to store many more positions than a nonservo robot.

□ Both continuous path and point-to-point capabilities are possible.

□ Accuracy can be varied, if desired, by changing the magnitude of the error signal which is considered zero. This can be useful in "rounding the corners" of high-speed contiguous motions.

□ Drives are usually hydraulic or electric and use state-of-the-art servo control technology.

□ Programming is accomplished by manually initiating signals to the servo valves to move the various axes into a desired position and then recording the output of the feedback devices into the memory of the controller. This process is repeated for the entire sequence of desired positions in space.

Common characteristics of servo-controlled robots include:

□ Smooth motions are executed, with control of speed and, in some cases, acceleration and deceleration. This permits the controlled movement of heavy loads.

□ Maximum flexibility is provided by the ability to program the axes of the manipulator to any position within the limits of their travel.

□ Most controllers and memory systems permit the storage and execution of more than one program, with random selection of programs from memory via externally generated signals.

□ With microprocessor or minicomputer-based controllers, subroutining and branching capabilities may be available. These capabilities permit the robot to take alternative actions within a program, when commanded.

□ End-of-arm positioning accuracy of 1.5 mm (.060 in.) and repeatability of ± 1.5 mm (± .060 in.) are generally achieved. Accuracy and repeatability are functions of not only the mechanisms, but also the resolution of the feedback devices, servo valve characteristics, controller accuracy, etc.

□ Due to their complexity, servo-controlled robots are more expensive and more difficult to maintain than non-servo robots and tend to be somewhat less reliable.

Point-to-point servo-controlled robots. One subset of the servo-controlled robot class is the point-to-point robot. This is the typical servo-controlled robot which is used in a wide variety of industrial applications for both parts handling and tool handling tasks. Significant features of the point-to-point servo-controlled robot are:

□ For those robots employing the "record-playback" method of teaching and operation, initial programming is relatively fast and easy; however, modification of programmed positions cannot be readily accomplished during program execution.

□ Those robots employing sequencer/potentiometer controls tend to be more tedious to program; however, programmed positions can be modified easily during program execution by adjustment of potentiometers.

□ The path through which the various members of the manipulator move when traveling from point to point is not programmed or directly controlled in some cases and may be different from the path followed during teaching.

Common characteristics of point-to-point servo-controlled robots include:

□ High-capability control systems with random access to multiple programs, subroutines, branches, etc. provide great flexibility to the user.

□ These robots tend to lie at the upper end of the scale in terms of load capacity and working range.

□ Hydraulic drives are most common, although some robots are available with electric drives.

Typical point-to-point servo-controlled robots manufactured or marketed in the United States include ASEA, Cincinnati Milacron, Pacer, Unimate, and Versatran.

Continuous path servo-controlled robots. The second subset of the servo-controlled robot class is the continuous path robot. Typically, the positioning and feedback principles are as described previously. There are, however, some major differences in control systems and some unique physical features. The significant features of the continuous path servo-controlled robot are:

- During programming and playback, data are sampled on a time base, rather than as discretely determined points in space. The sampling frequency is typically in the range of 60 to 80 Hz.
- Due to the high rate of sampling of position data, many spatial positions must be stored in memory. A mass storage system, such as magnetic tape or magnetic disc, is generally employed.
- During playback, due to the hysteresis of the servo valves and inertia of the manipulator, there is no detectable change in speed from point to point. The result is a smooth continuous motion over a controlled path.
- Depending upon the controller and data storage system employed, more than one program may be stored in memory and randomly accessed.
- The usual programming method involves physically moving the end of the manipulator's arm through the desired path, with position data automatically sampled and recorded.
- Speed of the manipulator during program execution can be varied from the speed at which it was moved during programming by playing back the data at a different rate than that used when recording.

Continuous path servo-controlled robots share the following characteristics:

- These robots generally are of smaller size and lighter weight than point-to-point robots.
- Higher end-of-arm speeds are possible than with point-to-point robots; however, load capacities are usually less than 10 kg (22 lbs.).
- Their common applications are to spray painting and similar spraying operations, polishing, grinding, and arc welding.

Typical continuous path robots manufactured or marketed in the United States include ASEA, Binks, Retab, Trallfa, and Versatran.

Interfacing

Every application requires that the robot interact with something in the execution of its programmed task. Even a simple part transfer operation cannot be successfully accomplished without a part available for the robot to handle or until the robot has been signaled that the part is present. Interfacing the robot and related equipment involves the transmission of information in two directions. A common robot application, spotwelding of an automobile body, will serve to illustrate the extent to which interfacing may be required.

As the automobile enters the robot work station, its body style is determined and this information is sent to the robot for selection of the proper program to be executed. When the body is in place in the work station, this condition is sent to the robot so that it can begin to work. When the robot has manipulated the welding gun into its first programmed position, it sends a signal to the weld control to initiate the spotwelding process. When the spotweld is made, the weld control sends a signal back to the robot. The robot then manipulates the spotweld gun to the next programmed position and again signals the weld control. This process continues until the welding has been completed. When the robot has then moved clear of the body, it sends a signal to the conveyor and the automobile is moved out of the work station.

Similarly, branching can be initiated during the execution of a program by transmission of the appropriarte signal to the robot. In a transfer operation, for example, if the location into which the robot is to place a part is already occupied, a signal may be used to interrupt the normal program and branch to a program which directs the robot to an alternative location to dispose of the part.

Moving line operations, either those involving multiple axis line tracking or pacing of the line with the robot on a transporting device, require the interfacing of the robot and the line. In this case, a resolver/tachometer or encoder feedback device driven by the line provides a continuous flow of position and velocity information to the robot. By this means, the robot maintains synchronization with the work while it moves along the line.

Another area of interfacing is the provision of sensory feedback to the robot. One common application is in destacking material. Here, a tactile sensor is mounted on the tool with which the robot handles the parts. The robot is programmed to advance its arm in the direction of the stack, with the programmed stopping point beyond the last piece in the stack. When the sensor contacts a part, its signal interrupts the program, stops the advance of the arm, and activates the tool. The program then continues on the next step, removing the part from the stack. This type of sensory feedback is applicable to both nonservo and servo-controlled robots. Other types of sensors, such as proximity detectors, force feedback, and vision systems, may also be applied to robots in a similar manner.

Conclusion

As described here, all robots share some common characteristics. However, they vary greatly in complexity and capability. The complexity of a robot bears a direct relationship to its total ability; the more universal its applicability, the more complex a robot becomes. The trend of robotics is toward greater capability and flexibility and, as a result, greater complexity.

Centralized control of groups of robots by large computers, perhaps integrated into total manufacturing systems, is under investigation. Greater application of sensory feedback, particularly through the use of low-cost vision systems, is a reality today. Off-line programming by means of computers which may include interactive graphics systems is being explored.

While all of these developments will enhance its capabilities and apparent complexity, the robot will remain a basically simple device. Mechanical designs will follow conventional practices; servo control likewise will be conventional and controllers will utilize state-of-the art technology. Thus, the basics of robotics, once mastered, will not become obsolete.

General Conclusions

We began our discussion of the computer-integrated factory by saying that the technology exists today to make tomorrow possible. We also stated that the process would be evolutionary. Many "modules" for this exist. It only remains to apply the will to put them together. □ *Chester Gadzinski*

MATERIALS MANAGEMENT

Materials management represents an attempt to reach a balance between conflicting interests through the planning and control of materials from acquisition through manufacturing to the finished product available for sale. The primary concerns of materials management are adequate supply to maintain satisfactory customer service levels, economic utilization of plant equipment and labor, and optimum dollar investment in materials. As materials costs in many operations account for approximately four times the labor costs of converting these materials to finished product, it becomes increasingly important to maintain a high degree of control over investment inventories.

Functions

Materials management is often an opportunity to organize related functions under one manager to provide increased control and avoid wasteful overlapping of activities. Among these functions are planning, production control, inventory control, scheduling, purchasing, stores, receiving, warehousing, shipping, materials handling, value analysis, statistical analysis, traffic, operations research, make-or-buy decisions, distribution control, forecasting, and materials control. Actually, few organizations, if any, include every one of these functions.

Materials management today would include the following functions under the materials manager's direction: production planning; materials control; purchasing; traffic; receiving, handling, and shipping; and distribution control. There has been much controversy between production and inventory control, purchasing, and physical distribution over the question of which of them should dominate the materials management function. The answer lies in the effective integration of all key functions to meet the business needs of the company rather than the establishment of any dominant function.

The discussion below covers production planning and materials planning and control. Materials handling as a part of the materials management function generally consists of the receiving, warehousing, and shipping operations. Support for this area in the form of engineering studies and major equipment analysis is provided by the industrial or plant engineering departments. This subject is covered under materials handling and warehousing, later in this section. For details on purchasing, transportation, and physical distribution, see Section 5.

Organization and Place in Corporate Structure

If materials management is to provide top management with the control of materials supply, inventory investment, and flow-through operations that are its primary responsibility, it must have authority commensurate with that responsibility. Moreover, because they must coordinate and time activities between many unrelated areas, it is important that materials management personnel become proficient in communicating with a variety of persons concerned with specialized functions.

Materials management should be considered one of the major functions within the operation. It is generally a part of total operations responsibility and should report to the vice president/director of manufacturing or the president/divisional general manager.

Before the organization structure can be developed, specific decisions must be made on the functions to be included. A number of factors will undoubtedly influence this decision. Some of them are the complexity of the business, the importance of various functions within the present organization, the recognition of simple resistance to change, and the competence and availability of managerial talent. Other influences are the need for improved cooperation between functions, a requirement for tighter inventory control, and anticipated improvements in communication, coordination, and control.

The increased use of electronic data processing in volume manufacture, as essential to tight inventory control at high customer service levels, has introduced a level of integration in the manufacturing/materials planning and control process, so that policies and procedures are well disciplined: order policy, delivery policy, inventory months-of-supply, lot sizing, etc. The net result is that the predominant organization structure today controls materials from acquisition through manufacturing to finished-goods inventory.

Production Planning

Production planning is defined as "the function of setting the limits on levels of manufacturing operations in the future" (Dictionary of Production and Inventory Control Terms, American Production and Inventory Control Society, Chicago, 1966). The production plan establishes the ground rules that will be followed within the limits of previously determined corporate policies. The development of a plan will provide a forward look at inventory levels as they relate to inventory turnover and investment and cash-flow requirements, the degree of customer service that can be anticipated (based on planned stock positions), and the need to begin stockpiling inventories early to overcome seasonal sales patterns and limits in manufacturing capacity. Forward planning will determine the need to increase or decrease the labor force or attempt to maintain level employment through inventory planning. It provides the basis for authorization of actual manufacturing activities. Advance planning permits the orderly procurement of raw materials and components. It allows time for purchasing vendor selection, negotiation, and make-or-buy decisions.

The Sales Forecast

The sales forecast is the foundation on which all plans are based. The relative accuracy of the forecast will have a direct effect on future capital investments, inventory turnover, efficient utilization of equipment, and customer service. Unless the forecast provides a firm foundation for planning, much time, effort, and money will be misdirected.

Types of forecasts. Forecasts fall into three general categories: (1) long-range, projecting out five years and used for equipment planning and plant expansion; (2) medium-range, projecting out two years and used for the examination of seasonal patterns and the procurement of specialized production materials requiring long lead times; (3) short-range, projecting out 6 to 18 months and used in the development of master plans and the procurement of production materials.

Forecasting responsibilities. Certain basic functional responsibilities with regard to forecasting should be considered:

- Preparing the forecast is the responsibility of marketing, with advice from production planning and market research.
- Developing the master plan is the work of production planning.
- Monitoring the forecast for deviations and trends is the responsibility of production planning.
- Interpreting the deviations and making forecast corrections is done by marketing.
- Regulating materials flow to accommodate changes in the forecast is the responsibility of production planning and materials control.
- Alerting management of developing problems that result from forecast deviations and changes is the responsibility of production planning.

To fulfill these responsibilties there must be a high degree of communication and cooperation between marketing and production planning. Marketing should think not only in terms of dollars of sales but also of units to be sold. Variations in unit prices can have a decided effect on the relationship between dollars and units. Production planning should provide marketing guidelines to use in changing the forecasts and developing promotions as they relate to changing manufacturing conditions and lead times.

Approach to forecasting. In developing a forecast, the first consideration is normally given to the overall business forecast; this provides an overall look at the anticipated climate of the future as it applies to the particular business or perhaps to a specific group of products within the business. The next step is to begin looking at each item within the product group. This is necessary if correct materials planning and scheduling are to be achieved. At this point, historical, statistical trends, seasonality patterns, and changing promotional plans must be considered. Also, new-product introductions and their impact on existing products will need to be examined. Numerous advanced statistical techniques can be applied to the development of forecasts.

Forecast evaluation. Proper forecasting requires a specific procedure for routinely evaluating the forecast. Deviations from forecast must be examined and changing trends recognized. Statistical techniques can be utilized to establish control limits that indicate the significance of forecast deviations. There are two basic reasons for revising forecasts: (1) recognition of changing trends and patterns in the marketplace because of customer preference, competition, or other uncontrollable factors; (2) planned changes in promotional plans. Forecasts should be revised as soon as the first of these two conditions is recognized to be of significance; to ignore the condition and fail to begin rescheduling manufacturing activities to actual sales conditions can only lead to excess inventories or out-of-stock conditions.

Before changing forecasts under the second condition, it should be determined whether manufacturing lead times will permit timely support for the new promotional plan. Otherwise, a planned promotion may end with an out-of-stock condition, considerable customer dissatisfaction, and wasted promotion money.

Supply/Demand

The key input to the process of developing the master production plan is the sales forecast. However, there is a need for effective, integrated planning between marketing, manufacturing, and finance in order to arrive at the trade-off decisions that are required to balance manufacturing and finished-goods inventories in conjunction with other company resources. To develop the master production plan, it is necessary first to evaluate the market environment (see Figure 4-16) and to compare inventory position and schedule performance. It then becomes possible to make the compromises that are necessary to arrive at the "demand net requirements." This process is known as supply/demand.

The Master Production Plan

Periodically, the master production plan is prepared from the most recently updated "net demand requirements" and is, in fact, the manufacturing build schedule and production commitment. In general, because of manufacturing cycles and purchasing lead times, master planning should project at least a year. Planning for manpower, materials, machinery, and equipment should be based on the approved master production plan and, therefore, requires high accuracy. Since conditions will change, the frequency of the supply/demand process should accommodate the need for revision and will vary by business. Revisions are often prepared monthly and/or quarterly.

Certain steps should be considered in preparing the master production plan: (1) Determine how far forward the master production plan should project. (2) Establish the frequency with which the plan will be updated. (3) Establish the minimum inventory level acceptable for each product. This is the quantity below which the desired customer service levels cannot be met. (4) Establish some common measurement of products, units, and families of products. This will be nec-

Figure 4-16. Company inventory management for a multiplant machine assembly operation, as part of the company materials management function.

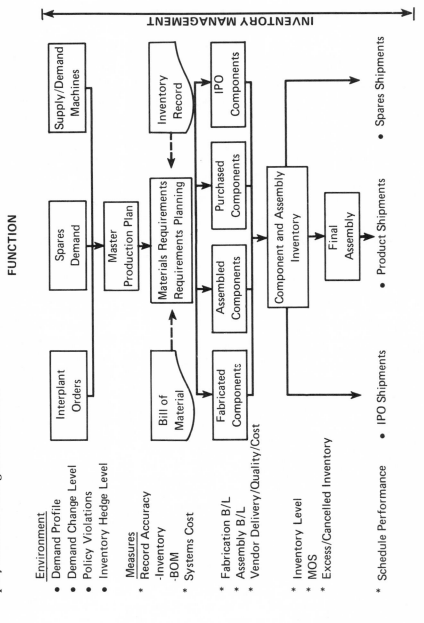

essary in order to relate production requirements to facilities and labor requirements. (5) Be certain that the sales forecast is stated in the unit of common measurement and broken down into time intervals. The forecast for production planning should be in units of each item to be sold during each time period. A forecast in dollars on an annual basis will not suffice. (6) Basing the calculation on inventory at the starting period and desired position, by month or quarter, spread the production requirements over the planning period. At this time, production leveling and capacity limitations by groups of products are taken into account and problem areas are identified in a general way. This plan will also provide a projection of inventory position and turnover rate throughout the year. (7) Analyze the data and determine the corrective action required to avoid potential trouble areas. (8) Establish controls that will identify variations between plan and actuality for sales and production. These controls should operate by exception so that only deviations of significance, justifying changes to the plan, will be highlighted. (9) Obtain high-level approval of the master production plan since it provides management with one of the key tools in running the business.

Detailed Planning and Scheduling

Detailed plans and schedules can be developed from the master plan; they must provide for the implementation and control of the master schedule in each of the various phases of manufacturing. Requirements for economic production quantities, a production authorization system, the development of machine loading data, and dispatching procedures will be set up.

Inventory policy. Inventory policy is essentially the balancing of investment in inventory against a desired customer service level. Too little inventory will cause out-of-stock conditions. Too much inventory will tie up funds that could be used for other purposes. There are four basic types of inventory:

Safety stock is inventory planned to take care of fluctuations in sales demand and manufacturing lead time.

Anticipation stock is inventory built up in advance of planned seasonal selling peaks, special promotions, or plant shutdowns. This planned buildup recognizes the capacity limitations of the manufacturing facility. This type of buildup should be planned to occur as close to the time of need as possible.

Economic order quantity (EOQ) stock is inventory planned by the use of mathematical formulas that have been developed to determine the most economic order quantity for any item to be manufactured or purchased. The use of this analysis provides an answer to the question of how much and how often to produce. It provides a balance between setup costs, manufacturing costs, and inventory carrying costs.

Distribution stock represents the amount of inventory that must be available to provide time distribution of the stock from the manufacturing plant to the warehouse and the ultimate customer.

Inventory categories. Manufacturing companies generally classify inventories in four categories: (1) *raw materials*—the materials that will be converted or combined during the manufacturing process; (2) *components*—the parts, subassemblies, and packaging materials that will become a part of the final product; (3) *work in process*—the materials worked on at various stages of the manufacturing process; and (4) *finished stock*—the final product ready for sale to the customer.

A useful practice in establishing inventory policy is to apply the ABC principle to each of these categories of inventory. This principle simply recognizes that, as a rule, 20 percent of all products represent approximately 80 percent of inventory investment. Each category of inventory can be broken down into three or more groups on the basis of their value. Different inventory policies and procedures can be applied to the A (high dollar) group and to the C group, which represents very little value. The most important products should be controlled more closely because they represent a greater dollar investment.

Machine loading and labor.   The production plan must be examined to determine whether sufficient labor hours are available and whether machine capacity is adequate. Labor requirements can be determined by applying the current established labor standard to the units of production required. A summary of labor hour requirements should be compared to the current actual output of the existing labor force coupled with productivity plans, as the basic measurement of current capacity.

Machine loading compares the quantity of work to be done on a machine or group of machines with the capacity and availability of the equipment. Short-term overloads on machines can be overcome by overtime or rerouting of work to other machines. Long-term overloads can be solved only by procuring additional equipment, changing production methods, or purchasing the item from an outside source.

Dispatching and marshaling.   Dispatching is the job of seeing that the plans and schedules are followed in the manufacturing area. This is done through the release of job or production orders. The manufacturing departments should produce only those items for which they have been given an order. The dispatching group will determine priorities and materials routing between departments, see that work is forwarded from one area to another, report idle time of machines and operators, and request action on delays. In some cases, timekeeping is also a responsibility of the dispatching function.

The marshaling movement of materials from the warehouse to the first process operation and from one operation to another is performed by the dispatching group. This frees the manufacturing supervisor from concern about materials availability and permits him to concentrate on efficiency of operation and quality of product.

Materials Planning and Control

To support the planned and scheduled manufacturing operation, it is essential that raw materials and components of the right type and quantity are available when needed. At the same time, excess inventories of these materials tie up dollars, reduce turnover, and present potential obsolescence problems.

Materials Order Systems

The type of order system used will depend to some extent on the size and complexity of the business. Frequently, several different systems are used concurrently for different types of materials that present distinctly different problems. One universal application is the ABC analysis of all materials; it provides the basis for setting up inventory policy on each category of materials. When this ranking of materials, based on dollar value, has been completed, the correct emphasis can be placed on each group of items and inventory investment can be controlled. For example, a commonly used screw representing an annual purchase of only $1,000 will be purchased once a year, while a specialized raw material representing annual purchases of $50,000 will be purchased on a monthly basis. Dollar investment, clerical control, and order costs are used to the best advantage.

In any order system, the lead time necessary for procuring additional supplies of an item must be considered. EOQ analysis should also be completed, along with the determination of price break points, based on purchase quantities, to determine how much of each raw material or component should be procured at each reordering point. Some of the order systems in use today are briefly described below:

The two-bin system. This is a simple system whereby a determined amount of stock is set aside (frequently in a separate bin or sealed bag). When all other stock has been used and this separate stock must be opened and used, an order is placed for replenishment stock.

The visual review system. Stock levels are checked visually and replenishment orders are placed when a predetermined minimum level is reached. This is a common application for tank-held items, because it is important that a new order not be placed for tank wagon delivery until there is sufficient room in the inventory holding tank.

The order-point system. This system is based on perpetual inventory records; when an item reaches a predetermined order point, a replenishment order is placed.

The materials control system. This system is the most sophisticated and, in medium-size or large businesses, is generally handled on electronic data processing equipment. In this system, orders for materials are based on a production plan. Quantities and delivery requirements are predetermined on the basis of safety stock factors, production requirements, economic order quantity analysis, and procurement lead times. Common materials for different finished-stock products are collated and summarized within specific time periods.

In recent years, MRP (materials requirement planning) has been implemented in many companies with multilevel product structure and multiplant operations. MRP can be the core system to an effective integrated planning process from demand through finished product. Figure 4-17 is a simplified illustration of a materials requirement planning system.

The master schedule, as described above in "Production Planning," is the key interface between marketing and manufacturing and, in effect, is the production commitment to a build schedule of time-phased end items that are required to satisfy the sales demand. This tells manufacturing what to build and when it should be completed.

The manufacturing bill of materials and configuration control is the interface with design engineering which converts the engineering bill of materials to the "as built" manufacturing bill of materials and maintains the configuration control

Figure 4-17. MRP (materials requirement planning).

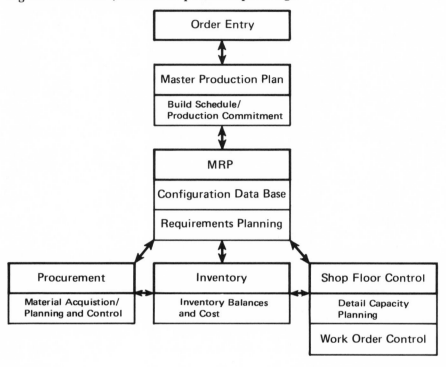

to handle engineering changes. This tells manufacturing how to build the product. The procurement, stores, and work-in-progress status reflects the on-hand and on-order inventory position.

Beginning with the master plan, MRP then explodes the top-level materials requirements level by level in accordance with the manufacturing bill of materials/product structure, combines the requirements of identical components, compares the current status to the gross requirements, and calculates the net requirements. The net requirements may then be adjusted for problem solving and potential economies, after which planned orders by time period are generated.

MRP superimposes a strict discipline on the materials manager and the other key functions. Properly executed, it can become an excellent vehicle for integrated planning within manufacturing, and between manufacturing and its key interfaces. At present, it is most effective with respect to materials acquisition, parts fabrication, and batch flow assembly. It has limitations with respect to continuous flow assembly lines, and a supplemental replenishment system is required to support continuous flow.

Safety Stock

The decision on how much safety stock to maintain for any category of materials is difficult and requires the attention of corporate management. With too much safety stock and poorly defined limits, excess inventory will result.

It is a natural tendency—at all levels—never to run out of stock and thus be safe. Most businesses cannot afford the luxury of never having an out-of-stock condition. Conversely, too frequent an out-of-stock condition will result in manufacturing interruptions and poor customer service. The determination of reserve stock is based on the accuracy of forecast demand, the size of the economic order quantities, the length and accuracy of lead times for procurement of materials, and the service level demanded.

A number of statistical techniques can assist in the determination of safety stocks. Two of these techniques are the estimation of forecast error and the calculation of reorder point by product based on probability of out-of-stock conditions.

Lead Time

The time to procure or manufacture an item must be identified. Lead time becomes a part of the planning and controlling activity if inventories are to be kept within required limits and materials are to be available on a timely basis to avoid work interruption. The introduction of new plant equipment can have a dramatic effect on lead times and consumption requirements. Changes in suppliers, general industry backlogs, and supplier operating problems and strikes can cause lead times to change. Through frequent contacts with supplier representatives, purchasing can identify changes in lead times for procurement. These changes must be communicated to the materials control function so that requisitions for materials will be placed on a realistic basis.

Physical Inventories

The common practice is to take a complete physical inventory of all production materials once each year. As a supplement to this and in some instances as an eventual replacement for the annual physical inventory, rotating or cyclical inventories are taken. When rotating inventories are taken, their frequency should be established on the basis of the value of various items. An ABC analysis should be made for all items. Those items representing the top 80 percent in value may be checked every three or four months. Those with very little dollar value would require checking only every two years.

The physical inventory provides an opportunity to verify and correct inventory records. Normally, two counts of each item are made by different people. The warehousing, stores, materials control, and accounting personnel generally conduct the count. An auditing team should also participate in the physical inventory.

New Techniques

Most of the methods and techniques discussed above have already been tried and proved and are in general use today. The dynamic evolution of rapidly increasing business complexity, the introduction of advanced computer technology, and the application of mathematical analysis have brought to the area of materials management a dramatic future. The potential applications of new methods must constantly be explored. Some of these are described briefly here.

Line of balance. A simplified technique developed to assist in the monitoring of various defense projects is line of balance. The concept is one of control by exception. It deals only with the main checkpoints that pertain to the overall project schedule. A basic reporting system rather than a detailed planning system, it simply attempts to monitor a project's progress as related to its planned goals. This technique is a simple monitoring tool to replace the knowledge and follow-up in a total situation that was once handled in a less complex situation by the line supervisor. The concept is related to PERT (Program Evaluation and Review Technique).

Line of balance is established in three phases and committed to graphic presentation for tracking. The three phases are (1) establish the basic delivery schedule and on the same chart plot the actual performance on a week-to-week or monthly basis; (2) establish the time and unit schedule, indicating how each major part of the total project will be completed; and (3) plot the progress of the manufacturing activity (taking into account purchased items and subassemblies) as of a certain date. The result is then compared to the original objective to determine the line of balance. The analysis provides data on portions of the plan that are ahead of objective, as well as those that are late.

Critical ratio scheduling. A technique for continuously reestablishing production priorities based on the latest information is critical ratio scheduling. It is of particular value when lead times are long, since there is increased opportunity for change in the lead time intervals. The development of critical ratio scheduling generally indicates that production orders will not be released to the manufacturing department until required. This probability is based on the premise that 50 percent or better of these requirements will change in priority.

The critical ratio or priority for scheduling is based on available stock, reorder quantity, standard lead time to manufacture, and manufacturing lead time remaining. It is a technique for precisely putting first things first.

Planner performance. Through the use of electronic data processing and the detailed explosion of requirement techniques against an established plan, it is now possible to determine individual planner performance.

By the use of an input of predetermined criteria such as safety stock, lead time to manufacture, test time, forecast, and inventory position, it is possible to prepare a theoretically ideal production plan. This plan can be modified by the individual planner proceeding from knowledge he possesses regarding anticipated changes in capacity, component delivery, or other factors. This exploded plan (broken down into finished stock, raw materials, and components) can be shown in terms of a dollar variance from the ideal plan. It will indicate dollars of inventory overcommitted or potential out-of-stock conditions. This technique will be of great assistance to management in monitoring individual planner performance.

Simulation theory. Through the use of computer programs, it is possible to simulate the consequences of planning and inventory decisions in terms of dollar investment in the future or potential out-of-stock conditions. When these techniques are fully developed, they will permit management decision experimentation before actual commitment. Ultimately, this should be an extremely useful tool in determining the best decisions for the business.

Evaluation of the Materials Management Function

To properly evaluate the materials management function, objectives must be established and understood by all levels of operating management. Many of these objectives in the area of inventory management and customer service are shared with other functional areas of management. These objectives must have the approval and support of corporate management if they are to be effectively attained. They should provide a good measurement of performance, and to do this they must be realistic and be thoroughly understood. Once these objectives are established, the following techniques and controls can be used to measure their attainment:

Inventory investment. A plan for the level of inventory investment should be established. This plan should project forward at least one year and take into consideration all special plans (buildups, major purchases, forecast sales, and production demands, for example) that are known. A monthly reporting system should be established to provide comparisons with previous years and projected plans. These reported data should be broken down by plant location, product groups, and types of inventory. The types of inventory covered should include raw materials, components, work in process, returned goods, and finished stock. This detail is necessary if problem areas are to be identified and the necessary corrective action taken.

Inventory turnover. Turnover data relating inventories to cost of sale and cost of materials used in production, for all categories, must be provided monthly. These data should be compared with a projected planned turnover rate by month and on a cumulative basis.

Budget control. A majority of costs associated with the materials management function are associated with fixed personnel costs. Comparisons should be made periodically with industrywide surveys to determine whether organizational staffing is reasonable. In recent years, the introduction of computer-oriented systems has provided an opportunity for reduction in clerical effort.

Customer service levels. Precise data should be accumulated in the area of customer service. Common goals in this area are expressed as a percentage of customer orders shipped incomplete and the percentage of line items that are backordered. Total backorders should be analyzed item by item, including not only the number of items and the dollars of backorder but also the length of time the item has been backordered. The operational area responsible for the backorder should be identified so that the necessary corrective action can be taken. This is extremely important, since many different areas of the operation can directly influence backorders and ultimate customer service levels.

Manufacturing efficiency. Frequently, manufacturing efficiencies and costs are affected by planning and scheduling activities. A detailed analysis of change-overs, idle time, and materials delays can indicate a need for improved planning and materials control activities.

Number of months of stock. The determination of the number of months' coverage of finished stock is a frequently used indicator of adherence to inventory plans.

Comparison of actual with planned production. Information on how well planning is being followed in actual practice is provided by this comparison.

Timeliness of promotions. A constant review should be made of the availability of stock to support special promotional plans and new-product introductions.

Forecast performance. Forecast versus actual sales should be regularly reviewed. This review should make allowance for required manufacturing lead times. For example, last month's actual sales should not be compared with a forecast introduced last month. These sales should be compared with a forecast introduced several months earlier, which allows time for manufacturing to react.

Disposal of assets. Obsolete and surplus materials that result in a disposal of assets cost should be monitored. An analysis of such costs should be kept by category of material, dollars to be disposed of, number of items, and reasons.

Stability of labor force. Frequent hiring and firing of the labor force add costs through training costs, operating inefficiencies, employment costs, and compensation costs. Wherever possible within the limits of inventory policies, effort should be made to maintain a level workforce through scheduling adjustments.

Warehousing costs. Failure to maintain proper inventory levels and dispose of obsolete materials regularly will soon add significantly to warehouse costs. This result is particularly noticeable when warehouse space is being rented.

Slow-moving items. Production planning should routinely identify, for marketing management, those products that are moving slowly and indicate potential obsolescence. This will provide an opportunity for special promotional plans for disposing of such materials.

□ *John F. Klizas* (*and* **L. Frank Edelblut,** *the original author of this now substantially revised section*)

MATERIALS HANDLING AND WAREHOUSING

Materials handling has been aptly described as the logistics of industry. It encompasses the movement of raw materials to the plant and through the processing cycle, and the delivery of finished goods to the customer through distribution channels. Whether the work-in-process material moves in a box, on a conveyor, or in a pipeline, the activity is still materials handling.

The manufacturing process may require hours or years, but at every stage—even when materials are stored between operations—the handling of materials should be performed by the best techniques possible. Although there have been many advances in processing machines, until recent years very little was done to recognize, analyze, and reduce the costs of the indirect labor of materials handling. Since handling adds nothing but cost to the product, the first goal is to eliminate handling whenever possible.

Good materials handling is imperative throughout the distribution system, for here the product is at its highest manufactured cost—completed, inspected, and packaged. If damage caused by poor handling occurs, the product must be returned and reworked at the factory or reworked, reinspected, and repacked in a less efficient field operation. If damage occurring in distribution is ignored or undetected, the worst penalty of all is applied—customer dissatisfaction. These are all cogent reasons for the development of the best handling and distribution system that can be devised.

Basic Handling Principles

It is basic to any handling operation that the movement of the material must keep pace with the needs of the operation (quantity) so that an out-of-stock condition never occurs. It must be done, however, with the least amount of damage and at the lowest practical cost.

Wherever possible, the force of gravity is used to move the material through the stages of processing. Liquids and granular dry materials are frequently stored in a vertical silo so that mixing, blending, or treating may proceed at stages of a natural flow from top to bottom by gravity. The goal is to keep materials at each stage instantly available for movement when needed without incurring further handling costs. This in-flow storage principle may be used in many other kinds of systems.

When high-volume movement, heavy loads, round-the-clock operations, or hazardous or unpleasant working conditions are involved, an automated mechanical system may be a good investment. If the payoff will not justify an automated system, a mechanical system with people at key points may be justifiable. Where short runs or variety of product or processing may preclude the use of all but the simplest of handling devices, carts, containers, universal conveyors, or general utility trucks and racks may suffice.

In terms of return on investment, a high-priced, automatic system may be the best buy if it eliminates enough labor. The cost of eliminating labor by mechanical operation varies greatly with the complexity of the handling operation. Usually, mechanical handling is cheaper, causes less damage, and is much safer than manual handling.

Layout

The layout of facilities is generally dictated by the dominant factors in any materials-handling system—the materials, the building, the method, the available funds. If a system is being created from scratch, the receiving department should be planned so that truck or rail movement will not interfere with employees' or visitors' access to parking lots or buildings.

A "quality hold" storage area adjacent to the receiving station must be adequate to permit the retention of incoming materials long enough for sampling, testing, and palletizing or preparing the stock for movement to the storage areas.

Ideally, the stock would now be in suitable containers and in typical quantities to serve the production line so that it could be moved to a position adjacent to the area where it would be used. Storage of incoming materials *at the point of use* does more than just eliminate waiting-for-stock downtime. It minimizes handling labor and helps to monitor overordering while serving as a visual reminder of depleted stock at the reorder point.

If floor storage is decided upon, both raw stock and in-process storage may be allocated to the wall areas that will be moved out in the event of plant expansion. If such storage is along the expansion wall, many entrances and handling innovations may be added to keep pace with technological changes. If plant expansion occurs, it usually provides the best way to expand without shutting down production lines.

At the end of the production lines, there is usually an inspection area for quality testing and a packaging area. If packaging is done mechanically, the area should be large enough to allow for the newer, faster—but larger—machines which are the trend of the times. An adequate storage area for packaging materials should be planned adjacent to the point of use in the packaging area.

Loading facilities for rail and truck should be so planned that they provide ready egress from the plant area without creating traffic problems for personnel and vehicles. If the volume is high, a trailer park for both empty and full trailers should be provided so that tractor jockeying and other movement will not inhibit the loading cycle.

In the layout of a new facility, the process, equipment, storage, and handling are all planned, and then an architect is instructed to "wrap a building around it."

When a layout is planned for an existing building or process, compromises must be made. Frequently, the objective of having the best materials handling system must give way to some other dominant factor such as space requirements, building limitations, or process demands.

Equipment

Materials-handling equipment is offered in a wide variety of designs and capacities at, of course, wide variations in price. It is most important that its selection be properly made. Dependence on a salesman's word alone is not the best criterion for the selection of equipment that must fit the job. Errors at this point can be disastrous later on. If price is a great consideration, certain calculated risks can be taken, or a leasing plan may be considered rather than the purchase of basically unsuitable equipment.

If no one with sufficient handling equipment background is available within the company, by all means employ a consultant of known skill in the area being considered. A consultant has usually studied the particular usage in depth and can bring to the problem the wisdom of broad experience with almost any aspect of every handling job.

When new and untried designs are being considered, they may frequently be purchased with a performance guarantee whereby the risk in trying new equipment may be reduced.

If the performance of handling, packaging, or unitizing equipment is crucial to the production level, it is wise to provide for an alternative path and equipment (sometimes rental equipment) to maintain the flow if serious problems of any duration develop.

Methods

Handling methods are determined mainly by the type of material, the volume to be handled in a given time segment, and the percentage of return expected from the expenditure; but there are other considerations.

Marketing considerations can supply the ground rules as to whether the product will continue at high volume or whether design changes will be required to hold the sales volume. Engineering may be able to anticipate design or process changes that will influence the methods of handling to some extent.

If the process seems to have a long period ahead without change in design or volume, a high degree of mechanization or even automation is in order. If the trend is toward change, or if extreme versatility is one of the requirements, the methods are more likely to be simple, even manual. If equipment is used, the payoff must be scrutinized carefully.

Versatility and adaptability are likely to rank higher than efficiency in the selection of methods and equipment when change is imminent or likely. In such cases, people will probably dominate the operation, and there will be more reliance on human judgment. Controls will be more manual, and dependence on skilled personnel a greater factor. In such a simple system, controls may account for only 25 to 30 percent of the cost of the system. A sophisticated, highly automatic system can easily involve additional control costs of 50 to 75 percent of the cost of the mechanical system.

Production efficiencies for some expensive production machines may decline markedly for reasons of inefficient feeding or lack of materials. Some high-cost equipment is dependent upon operation 24 hours a day to provide an adequate return on the investment, and human failure may prevent an adequate return.

Pacing the machine feeding or other operations by the insertion of mechanical conveyors can often restore the feed rate needed. To hitch the human being to the machine pace may require some orientation, but it frequently results in greater employee satisfaction because the pace is more rhythmic. Many conveyors are supplied with variable speed controls for just such reasons.

Manpower

To determine manpower requirements, an analysis must be made of the flow of raw materials, work in process, and finished stock through the manufacturing operation. This analysis should include volumes and scheduling patterns. Common techniques such as time study and work sampling can be applied to determine manpower requirements. The number of units or pallets moved per hour is a meaningful measurement in evaluating manpower requirements.

Materials-Handling Equipment

The range of materials-handling equipment includes conveyors and vehicles of many kinds for the horizontal movement of materials; cranes, hoists, and elevators for vertical movement and storage; and containers and supports.

Conveyors

Conveyors are frequently used to move loose powdered, granular, and solid materials as well as packaged materials in containers. A few years ago, many of these were designed to fit a specific need and were not available except on special order. Today their proliferation is extended to accessories and modular unit design that permits the insertion of added sections so that the conveyors can grow with the layout.

Some equipment manufacturers specialize in package conveyors, others in bulk material conveying; it is worthwhile to seek vendors who have experience in what the problem requires.

Cranes, Hoists, Elevators

Cranes are made mobile for outdoor use on almost any kind of terrain and are made very versatile for yard storage and handling by the accessories available. They may be equipped with magnetic or mechanical grabs that make random pickup or rack stacking very simple. Counterbalanced reach forks enable steel bars, pipe, lumber, and other materials to be stacked or retrieved from vertical racks for very efficient storing and picking. Cranes for inside use are made mobile and sized to fit almost any need.

Overhead rail cranes are offered in a great variety of sizes and capacities and can be operated from the floor by a control pendant. Wireless controls are also available; they operate the crane by radio signals from a small box on the operator's belt. Such controls have increased the hours of effective use and provide better crane service with safer operation.

Hoists have been so updated in design that continuous operation without operators is a reality, and vertical movement can be almost as simple as horizontal movement. These are available in sizes and capacities from small cartons to full pallet loads.

Where large shaftways were formerly required, hoists (vertical conveyors) are now available which, by ingenious design, require space not much larger than the loads to be carried. Formerly, reciprocating movement limited speeds because the return trip was empty; but now there are vertical conveyors that are continuous in operation and can convey at speeds matching that of horizontal conveyors. Such equipment needs no operator to ride the car and can be loaded and unloaded without additional labor by automatic conveyors. The elimination of operators has drastically reduced the cost of vertical materials handling.

When, in the course of horizontal materials flow on the factory floor, an aisle or other conveyor intervenes, the new design of continuous-flow vertical conveyors permits movement up and over the aisle without the penalties of slow speed and operator involvement.

A built-in feature of every multistory factory building in the old days was the freight elevator. Slow, with cumbersome safety gates, and requiring an operator, such vertical movement required in addition a man to load and a man to unload the car. The waiting time created a further waste of man-hours, thus making elevators a very expensive kind of vertical materials handling.

Freight elevators can now operate at higher speeds with automatically operated gates and other refinements that reduce operating costs. Some require only the deposition of pallet or other loads at a loading station adjacent to the elevator. The entire operation can be automatic and the loads unloaded on run-out conveyors which accumulate material loads on the proper floors.

A study of the load data and the direct and related costs of vertical materials handling will usually indicate the kind of equipment to buy.

Vehicles

Vehicles for the horizontal movement of materials range from straddle carriers, which can pick up 50-foot trailers or stacks of lumber of the same size, to single battery-operated scooters for personnel and materials.

Powered vehicles are available to move rail cars on a siding without waiting for the railroad locomotive. Personnel carriers have been improved to carry fire-fighting and maintenance equipment to the point of use. Telescopic ladders extendible to 60 feet or more are now moved to required locations through doorways and passageways no more than eight feet high.

Pushcarts and other manual traveling containers are now available for easier and even automatic dumping. Aluminum and magnesium are widely used as materials in their construction, which increases the volume per man while lowering the fatigue and accident factors.

Containers and supports

The movement of quantities of goods and materials from factory to customers and from plant to plant has been the subject of keen investigation. Starting with the Conex containers of World War II, the problems of protection from damage, weather, and pilferage have repeatedly found no better answer than containers.

Forty-foot trailers with built-in legs for support and removable bogey wheels and running gear are available. Suitable for rail, highway, air, and sea traffic, they are extremely versatile and can even be separated into 20-foot units. They can be stacked for storage in a yard or the hold of a ship and can be equipped with heating or refrigeration units.

Since road taxes are applied only to the wheel section (bogey), these storage boxes have possibilities for real economies. Taxes on inventory in many places are applied at a specific calendar time. Storage in containers that can be made mobile overnight represents the possibility of minimizing this form of taxation.

The savings in packing material, particularly in overseas shipment, are truly amazing when containers are used in lieu of the very expensive unit carton packing that is usually done. Packed and sealed in the factory, the container can be shipped overseas, and the next access to its contents will be by the consignee in some foreign country.

Similarly, domestic shipments of parts and subassemblies can be made plant to plant, obviating the need for much of the packing material and labor now required. In many instances, special containers can receive the parts in an oriented manner and feed them back in like manner to automatic machinery at their destination.

Specialized types of racks and racking are now obtainable "off the shelf" because their use is so general. Readily available are racks for cradling tires and storing coiled materials, steel drums, rugs and carpeting, and innumerable other unusual types of materials. The main purpose of such racking is to make easily available every separate type of article stored.

Racks to store pallet loads have reached a high stage of development; some rack systems are even being built first, and the building that will enclose them is added later. Racks are made that permit trucks to drive through the storage space to reach the distant filled spaces. Such racks will materially reduce the space wasted on aisles for access to stored materials.

Racks and racking systems are quite sophisticated; again, if there is no one on the staff who is proficient in this area, call in a consultant to design and plan the system.

Materials-Handling Systems

Modern industrial systems are very complicated; they are usually conceived and operated by teams that possess the skills of industrial engineers, production and inventory control specialists, production specialists, and materials handling experts. The system must be conceived in its entirety and consideration given to the impact of each specialty on every other phase of the production plan. Omissions and errors in the early planning show up as expensive obstacles to efficient production later.

Simulating the actual operation and its response to problems that normally arise is frequently performed on a computer to test the ability of the system to meet all obstacles and variations. By this technique the actual dollar cost of out-of-stock conditions, delayed shipments, and similar problems may be assessed in advance, and some prediction of their probability may be made before investment in a particular system is made.

Industrial Trucks

Many handling systems are based entirely on material movement by fork truck only. Such a trucking operation is very versatile, especially if it is coordinated and controlled by two-way radio mounted on the trucks.

Industrial trucks equipped with forks are the workhorses of industry, roughly nine times as efficient as the manual lifting and carrying of single-case loads. They are available with a remarkable array of special attachments to handle unusual loads with ease. Loads can be lifted by squeezing or hooking, by vacuum, by being pulled onto and pushed off forks; they can be rotated, compressed, and weighed while in transit. The possibility of damage to materials, however, is greater with fork trucks than with conveyors, and labor and maintenance costs are higher.

The ability to convey large, heavy loads with speed and versatility makes the fork truck method the most widely used in handling, particularly in warehousing.

Conveyor Systems

Conveyor systems are usually designed to connect fixed positions with the most appropriate type of conveyor (belt, roller, troughed belt, pan, plate, oscillating, air, and so forth), operated by gravity or powered. The speed at which they convey can be critical if the production line they feed is closely integrated. Frequently, the conveying speed is used to pace the production machine operators to obtain higher production rates.

In a closely integrated system, several slower production machines may be needed to keep up with a higher-speed machine in the next operation. The conveyors may be branched out to feed the multiple setup and converged again to feed the higher-speed equipment.

When a production machine is temperamental or has critical adjustments that tend toward excessive downtime, alternative paths through duplicate machinery should be built into the system.

Many methods are available to accomplish the switching of product flow through these conveyors—air, hydraulic, electrical, controlled by sonic or optical sensors.

A production system keyed to automatic conveying will usually be totally nonproductive if the conveyor system fails. If preventive maintenance is scheduled regularly, such failures will be very unlikely to occur.

Overhead conveyors. Manufacturing space is usually high-priced; it is natural to look overhead for the location where conveyors can connect floor-mounted equipment. Frequently, in older plants, it is the only remaining clear space where conveyors can be located.

When planning for overhead conveyor runs in a new building, it is wise to have all piping, ductwork, bus duct, or other overhead impediments run parallel to the production line or to the proposed conveyor line. The use of "air rights" within the plant may offer great returns because of the straight paths that are offered and the use of otherwise wasted space.

Overhead conveyors may be of many types similar to floor-mounted designs, with the exception of oscillating conveyors. These are not usually used overhead, because of the extra steel required to support and balance them as well as the live load they can create. Overhead monorail conveyors are uniquely suitable, because of their versatility, for carrying large or small objects of many shapes. Designs are available which permit raising and lowering the material loads, storage banks with automatic pickup and discharge, powered and free sections to rationalize out-of-phase production equipment, and automatic dispatching and pickup.

Overhead conveyors can be enclosed with safety screens that are easily released for conveyor servicing while completely protecting personnel and equipment below. Maintenance can be simplified by automatic lubrication systems and by automatic signaling systems that pinpoint troubleshooting problems. Some processes, such as washing, drying, painting, heating, cooling, seasoning, and storage, can often be included in a good overhead system.

Impact of Volume

Generally, large-volume, continuous handling in a process industry can be done so much more cheaply by a handling system that the savings can pay for sturdy, well-designed equipment replete with controls and maintenance provisions that mean low-cost, trouble-free operation over a long time period. In fact, the system may dictate the shape of the building and layout. Materials handling provisions not properly organized can raise costs to a prohibitive level and can even destroy production scheduling.

Large-volume production systems dependent upon manual handling and feeding run the risks of labor shortages, sickness epidemics, labor problems, and oversupply of labor during downtime. Virtually all of these risks can be eliminated by automatic conveyorized handling.

In a low-volume processing industry, simple gravity conveyors may have to suffice with in-process storage before each successive operation. This usually requires more floor space and better production scheduling and increases the investment in in-process materials. Sometimes, specialized containers are needed to make the system work or to prevent damage to the product.

Such conditions are typical of a job-shop operation. The versatility of the equipment is usually accompanied by a loss of efficiency and a higher labor content. Preservation of batch identity requires more record keeping.

Planning the Warehouse

In addition to the problem of locating the warehouse where transportation costs, land investment, taxes on stock, and labor costs are minimal, many other considerations are important. Hazards of weather such as high winds, flooding, tornadoes, and the like must be considered.

The degree of mechanization or automation of the warehouse facility is a most important decision, for it determines the design of the building. Many existing buildings are totally unsuited to mechanical warehousing because the column spacing and truss height (optimum, 35–40 feet) do not permit economical spacing of the aisles and mechanism.

If the volume is high and a single modular size (unit load) will accommodate most of the products, it will be worthwhile to consider a mechanized system. Most mechanized systems are basically a set of racks to store the modular loads with a storing and retrieving device that gives access to all loads. The system may also have a unit load makeup device (palletizer) and feed conveyors, strapping equipment, and so forth.

In general, the cost of constructing a high building is less than the cost of spreading out the greater area (two to three times greater) of a conventional warehouse. Labor savings are made in the automatic or mechanical storage and retrieval of product.

The alternative to this is, of course, the use of forklift trucks or other handling devices suitable for stacking loads (optimum, 21–24 feet high).

To minimize long runs by fork truck, some warehouses have a circulating tow-cart system powered by either an overhead or in-floor tow line. Fork lift trucks then do the handling of loads into trucks and rail cars from the tow-line carts. Electrically guided, self-powered tractors are also used to tow trains of carts. Automatic dispatching and guidance are a feature of most of these systems.

Location and Layout

Warehouse buildings are usually located adjacent to a rail siding and a good service road for trucks and trailers.

Sales offices and visitors' parking are usually located in the front of the building; the front entrance is as imposing as costs permit. Employee parking is usually at the sides or back to lessen confusion. Rail siding and out-shipment truck dock are usually located at right angles to the rear or sides of the building. This provides for minimum distance when some loads are transferred directly from one shipping mode to another.

If possible, rail sidings are extended beyond the building to provide more car capacity with the use of some car-moving device. If the rail siding is indoors, it removes the problem of "spotting" the cars with their doors at the warehouse doors. Truck docks are usually external, with weather-sealing door pads and mechanical dock boards to adjust to tailgate heights. Roll-up doors minimize heat and cold interchange during loading and unloading. Staging areas are arranged in a clear space before the rail and truck dock areas. Aisles are usually laid out in the direction of the longer axis of the building, with cross aisles at intervals for convenience. Sprinkler controls and lighting panels should be located at aisle ends for easy access without waste of space.

Bulk and Reserve Storage

Stock that is received or shipped in bulk can be stored in orderly piles on the floor or in piles separated in usable stacking height on pallets. Usually, access from one aisle is provided with stacks of a size that permits shipment within a reasonable time to approximate first-in, first-out shipping. Reserve storage may be similarly "brick stacked" for periodic feeding up to an order-selection area as required.

Internal Materials Flow

Basically, the flow of materials within a warehouse should be planned so as to minimize movement and handling. An analysis of previous orders will yield data on the quantity and frequency of each product; these data can be used to arrange the stock. The national average indicates that 15 percent of the products account for 85 percent of the traffic.

The 15 percent of products in high demand should be stored in closest proximity to the out-loading points. The quantities contained in unit loads should approximate the typical order quantity, if possible. Products in high demand could be received by truck or rail and reloaded directly in one move for out-shipment. Sometimes they can remain in the same conveyance with other products added to the load. Such treatment will definitely minimize handling.

Operations

In planning for the operations of a warehouse, consideration is given to the location of the order-filling area, methods of stock selection, shipping techniques, shipping and receiving docks, administrative offices, and service areas.

Order-filling areas.   The section most convenient to the order-staging area should contain a variety of the 15 percent of stock most frequently ordered, in ample quantity for picking small-lot and single-carton orders. These may be arranged in shelving or palletized in pallet racks for quick access. The next adjacent area should contain the unit loads and bulk stock of the items of highest frequency in quantity orders. Slow-moving items should be stored peripherally in quantities appropriate to their historical ordering quantity. Small-size cartons of fast-moving items can be stored in pick racks (supermarket slide racks) that permit wide selection in a small frontal area to reduce walking. They do require labor for stock replenishment to be effective. Order-picking forklift trucks make upper levels of pallet racks easily available for order picking also.

Stock selection methods.   Orders printed by computer frequently have the stock location printed out at the same time. The location of break bulk stock, at least, can be so indicated.

Because break bulk stock selection is time-consuming, it is frequently the starting point in order filling, leaving bulk and unit loads to be picked last.

The location of highest-frequency stocks may be changed by reason of seasonal demands, making permanent location of bulk stock impossible. Such changes should be posted to avoid confusion.

Labeling and other identification methods have much to do with speed in order picking. Large numbers, legible to a man with ordinary vision at a distance of 20 feet, will be very helpful. Product-numbering codes that give a clue to the classification of the product will aid in locating stock. This practice can also reduce the number of digits the stock man must remember, thus reducing errors in stock selection. Adequate lighting (minimum, 20 foot-candles), particularly in the aisles, will speed up order picking and reduce errors.

Shipping techniques.   Unit loads are frequently loaded first because the empty vehicle provides more space to maneuver. Side shifter forks are valuable in loading a tight load with minimum voids.

Manual loading should be done in such a manner that dunnage (space fillers) will be minimal if needed at all. Careful loading will prevent much of the transit damage, particularly in rail traffic. Mechanical dunnage, load-restraining devices, and special types of cars will do much also to ensure safe delivery of products. Obviously, heavy loads should be placed at the bottom when loading, and frail packages or cartons at the top.

Shipping and receiving docks.   The physical facilities for receiving and shipping from truck docks should have padded weather seals on the doors, mechanical dock levelers, and in-car lighting from the door frames.

Truck-leveling devices to raise or lower truck and trailer bodies are very useful and save time. (Some fork trucks have small floor clearance and cannot enter a truck body until it is almost level with the dock.)

Rail docks are usually at the same height as the floor of the car, and the open space is bridged with a dock board. Aluminum or magnesium dock boards with raised sides and gridded surface will make car loading easier and safer. Use of lightweight materials may prevent a hernia or crushed foot in the course of moving from one location to another. A mechanical railcar door opener is a "must" for safety reasons. In-car lighting can be accomplished conveniently with a variety of fixtures now available. Car loading is not only safer in a well-lighted car; damage to the product is usually lessened as well.

Administrative offices. The administrative offices should provide a view— from a picture window, if necessary—of a broad area of the warehouse such as the out-loading or order-marshaling area. A view down one aisle is not of very great help.

Service areas. A fork truck or conveyance-repair area should be provided, usually close to the battery-charging area if electric trucks are used. If liquefied petroleum gas trucks are used, check the insurance company's safety requirements for the storage and changing of gas cylinders.

Providing an area near the truck docks with a toll phone, coffee machine, and rest room will alleviate the problem of truckers' using company phones or wandering around in the warehouse.   □ *George C. Stryker*

QUALITY MANAGEMENT

Quality is everyone's responsibility, from the chief executive to those at the lowest level of the organization. Quality means conformance to standards or requirements, not glitter or gloss, not luxury or beauty. The function of a quality organization is to assure product performance, or conformance to requirements or standards. Standards of performance are set by management and are based on management's interpretation of the demands of the marketplace. Increasing attention is being given to quality as an integral part of strategic planning to improve market share and to compete with the growing pressures of foreign competition in world and domestic markets.

Role of the Quality Control Director

Today's quality control director reports to top management rather than to the production manager, and he has other responsibilities than those of testing, rejecting, and approving. His responsibility extends to participation in planning new products, production facilities, and manufacturing methods. He must also inform management of the long- and short-term impact of decisions affecting product quality, and must act independently as the conscience for the company.

Many highly successful companies consider the quality control function as a basically scientific discipline and therefore have its director report to the research director. This policy has the danger of insulating the quality function from day-to-day activities and making multilevel cross-communication with supervision more difficult.

Staff Requirements

The multidisciplinary nature of quality management calls for the utilization of people of diverse skills and backgrounds. Depending on the industry and the product line, quality staff may include chemists, engineers, inspectors, statisticians, pharmacists, and physicists. In specialized industries quality staff members may have backgrounds in pharmacology, physiology, bacteriology, biochemistry, or other sciences. People hired for their technical qualifications are candidates for training in the quality philosophy and management techniques. On the other hand, a quality control person hired for his management ability may require additional training in one or more of the specialized fields. In addition to on-the-job training, many universities and management training organizations offer excellent courses in the philosophies, objectives, and techniques of the quality control function.

As in any other discipline one of the most important keys to improving the performance of quality control personnel is a searching, realistic, and regularly scheduled performance appraisal. In conducting performance appraisals the objective should be improvement rather than merely measurement.

Multiplant Operations

In a large corporation operating at many locations or comprising many organizational units at one location, quality control may be centralized in one division or decentralized in the various operating units. Many successful large companies have recently taken the latter approach, appointing a quality manager for each operating unit and placing the responsibility for policy with a manager of corporate quality. To assure the adherence of decentralized quality units to corporate policy, periodic audits of each unit are made by the staff of corporate quality.

Control of Vendor Quality

One of the basic elements in the overall scope of quality control is vendor control, or vendor quality management. Without supplies that conform exactly to the specified requirements, the end product cannot conform to the established standards.

Vendor Selection

The responsibility of vendor selection rests with the design and purchasing elements of the organization. Selection, however, is only one part in the relationship between supplier and purchaser. Designers typically have the knowledge of who in industry has the technical capability to supply materials, but they do not always have access to information regarding their schedule performance, financial status, process controls, and capability. Therefore, it is imperative for a company to establish a formal system of supplier approval.

To begin with there are two areas of supplier approval: management systems and hardware systems. Each of these must be reviewed and approved before a customer can have confidence that a supplier has both process (hardware) capability and the personnel capability to manage it.

Review of the management system consists of an audit to determine if major system elements are firmly in place and part of the company's management.

Process capability is determined by a product qualification, or first piece verification, during which materials are subjected to tests to verify conformance to design requirements. Should any parameter fail to meet its requirements, a review of product and process is performed to determine the cause of the failure. If it is determined that the product has been overspecified, it is essential that a formal change be implemented in the requirements. Never leave changing requirements to chance; make certain that when complete, the product exactly conforms to requirements.

Once it has been determined that a supplier has the capability, the next step is to assure consistent reproduction of the first article.

Incoming Material

Nonconforming incoming quality of materials can generate increased costs to the purchaser in many ways. The first and most frequent result is an increase in inspection cost. If a sequential plan is used, an excessive number of defects will result in the inspection of a larger sample and may require 100 percent inspection. If the inspection is complex, and particularly if chemical, physical, or biological analysis is required, the cost of the inspection is substantial. Poor vendor quality practices may force the buyer to carry a large inventory to compensate for increased inspection time, rework, or on-line rejections.

Purchasing Relationship

Major benefits from the control of vendor quality result from a day-to-day working relationship between purchasing and the quality control function, which may be either formal or informal; in either case, it is important to remember that other functions in the purchaser's organization are involved. These include departments engaged in developing and setting specifications, such as the packaging, process engineering, and operating departments.

It should be the responsibility of purchasing to see that each vendor has complete specifications for each item; negotiations with the vendor on specifications should be conducted by purchasing with quality and other groups concerned, as required. Establishing firm criteria with suppliers before the fact is mandatory.

Vendor Quality Evaluation

Close cooperation between purchasing and quality control has become mandatory in the evaluation of a vendor's performance in quality, price, and delivery. The first step in this evaluation is a joint effort by purchasing, quality control, and the materials manager to rate vendors on quality and ability to meet delivery dates. This rating is subject to revision to reflect significant changes in vendor performance.

The basis for this rating or measurement system can be any unit of measure that reflects the vendor's actual performance. Such measurement not only should rank vendors but should communicate standards and requirements. It should moreover establish a basis for the manager to decide when and to what extent corrective action is necessary.

One such measurement system, which establishes a common base for all supplied materials to be measured, is parts per million (PPM), used extensively in Japan and increasingly in the United States. This type of measurement system, which is very useful in medium- and high-volume production, has also been used successfully in all ranges of vendor performance measurement. The principle behind PPM is that all recorded defects are projected on a million-part basis. That is, if 5,000 parts are received and it is found that there are 12 defective, the projected rating would be 2,400 PPM defective. If all materials received are extended in this same fashion, regardless of lot size, a relative order of priorities can be set. These priorities will then indicate to the purchaser where to concentrate corrective action to gain the maximum benefit from the vendor defect prevention program.

Organizing In-Process Controls

A company must recognize that it is always far less expensive to prevent defects than it is to correct them after they occur. The complex nature of the products of industry today makes it increasingly difficult to ensure that the product will be satisfactory if the only testing is on the final product. Process controls must be established to reduce costs by preventing defects, thereby avoiding expensive separation costs at the end of the production process.

Meeting the specifications for the end product is the result of a well-controlled program. This the the target which must be hit, and in-process control is the best means of increasing the probability of hitting it. Complexity of product design generates increased necessity for precision in testing. If quality judgment is based entirely on the final product, complete disassembly or destructive testing may be required.

In complex assemblies, one department may be the supplier to another which acts as the customer; in this instance, in-process controls must be used to determine the suitability of a part or an assembly for the next production step. In-process controls must therefore be developed for the whole process so as to test critical properties at critical points. Poor planning of in-process controls may result in meaningless measurements taken at inappropriate points in production. A smoothly functioning quality engineering organization must specify not only the measurements to be taken and the limits on them but also the specifications for each measurement device. The accuracy and sensitivity of the device must be keyed to the dimensions to be measured and the limits placed thereon.

Line Relationships

As part of the planning and in-process control, once the parameters and specifications have been set, production must be held responsible and accountable for enforcement. Quality control must monitor, audit, measure, and report on compliance. Since controlling in-process quality is a production tool, it must be the responsibility of the production unit. This is usually the case in mechanical and continuous-process industries, since there is no batch or other cutoff point where production can be halted and samples taken for examination by quality control.

Process Control Charts

Graphic representation of quality characteristics is a time-honored method of presenting information on in-process quality. Recent progress, which has increased the content of process control charts, has been greatly stimulated by automatic equipment for acquiring, logging, analyzing, and plotting quality characteristics. Computer programs are available to handle in-process control data, whether in terms of variable measurements or attributes. If attributes are used, established methods for classifying defects are available, as are statistical methods for determining the significance of deviations from the norm. These techniques have been developed because of the recognition that graphic presentation of quality information is much more easily assimilated than numerical presentation.

Inspection Reports

The dissemination of information obtained by in-process control is the key to its success. The type and extent of reporting depends on the recipient of the report. While detailed reports in tabular or graphic form may be required by those closely involved with production, the interest of management—including quality engineering and process development—is more likely to be in a brief summary of the current status. One very useful type of reporting is the exception report, which covers only the phases of the operation that are out of control. If in-process control is the responsibility of the production unit, then its exception reports to quality control, quality engineering, and process development serve as an indication that troubleshooting is required.

Final Testing

Theoretically, if in-process control or the prevention system is 100 percent effective, there will be no need for inspection or testing of the final product. If the product is a "single use" item, such as a rifle bullet or an intercontinental ballistic missile, final inspection and testing often cannot be done without destroying the product; complete reliance must be placed on in-process testing. Fortunately, the nature of many consumer products allows the testing of an adequate representative sample of the final product. If this is possible, the final inspection and testing confirm that the control of in-process quality has been effective.

Customer Feedback Information

Since the success of any product depends upon customer satisfaction, prompt attention must be paid to feedback of customer reaction to the product. There are many forms of customer reaction; it is important that they be recognized, properly routed, promptly evaluated, and answered. The most common form of feedback is a customer complaint, which may come directly to the company or may be forwarded by salesmen or field representatives.

Feedback from the Field

Salesmen are without doubt the best source of information on customer reaction and the product's relationship to competition. Analysis of customer complaints and replying to them are important functions of the quality organization, often supplemented by critical evaluation of the products of competition. Competitive evaluation is most effective when regularly performed, but may require additional attention when a problem arises.

The salesforce must be given detailed instructions on handling customer complaints; the importance of prompt communication through established channels must be emphasized. The staff in quality, charged with the responsibility of handling complaints, must be instructed in the importance of a rapid reply to the customer. A copy of the reply should always be sent to the representative handling the account. If replacement, refund, or credit is necessary, the proper people should be informed so that the adjustment can be made quickly and customer dissatisfaction dissipated.

Product Identity System

The system used to identify the product must be adequate to ensure thorough investigation of customer feedback. Such information as the model number, the serial or lot number, and the production date (the latter often keyed to the serial or lot number) is extremely important. If the complaint originates with a salesman, he must realize the importance of submitting as much specific information as he can obtain.

Failure Analysis

Failure of a product at the consumer level may be of several types. The product may be defective when received by the customer, or there may have been a weakness in design or construction that caused it to become defective in routine use. Another possibility is misuse by the customer.

If the product was defective when it reached the customer, it must be determined whether there was design failure, improper handling, or faulty manufacture. If design failure is to blame, correction should be instituted, since additional failures are likely. If manufacture was faulty, a weakness in the prevention system or the application of an unrealistic specification is a possible cause. If the complaint resulted from customer misuse, attention should be given to the directions for use of the product; these must be written so as to minimize misuse.

Another important aspect of the analysis of customer feedback is the evaluation of possible liability on the part of the manufacturer; if this is a possibility, the company's legal department should be made aware of the situation promptly.

Data Reporting System

In reporting information to management on customer feedback, the incidence of customer dissatisfaction should be related to the number of units produced; this is necessary to determine the severity of the problem. If a significant upward trend exists, the need for corrective action should be examined.

The classification of customer complaints often reveals geographic and seasonal differences, particularly if the product is adversely affected by extremes of temperature or humidity. Geographic differences in complaint incidence, particularly if the product is sold throughout the world, may reflect different uses (or misuses) of the product in different areas or different countries. Reports to top management should be limited to exceptional situations where management action or decision is required. Graphic presentation should be used wherever possible.

Corrective Action

Many types of corrective action may be taken in the light of customer dissatisfaction. These range all the way from a simple increase of the inspection effort to complete redesign of the product or the production facility. Wherever possible, quality control should include a recommendation for action in its report.

New-Product Development

The requirement of designing and building quality into a product has long been recognized. According to one of the oldest axioms in the field, "You cannot test quality into a product; you must build it in." Progress toward meeting this requirement was slow until the concept of total quality and the part played in it by quality engineering evolved in the years following World War II.

Quality engineering works with quality control, design engineering, and manufacturing engineering to plan product development. Its objective is to design a product that will be free of defects prior to the start of production.

In the absence of a quality engineering function, the key to satisfactory quality of new products is constant communication among all groups involved in new-product development. These may include research, process development, marketing, and, of course, quality control.

Interdepartmental Coordination

Quality engineering can act as a catalyst in obtaining required communication and interaction among all the groups involved in new-product development. It is most important to prevent the omission of important points and to resolve hangups quickly, and it is easier to take such action as product development proceeds than to go back and attempt to fill in gaps later.

CPM (critical path method) is a very useful tool for planning and scheduling product development. This method, correctly applied, serves as checklist, road map, schedule, and reporting system. It should be developed to show not only what needs to be done and when, but to indicate clearly to whom each responsibility is assigned. Programs are available for the use of computers as a follow-up and report system for CPM. The computer is programmed to print out regular progress reports, which raise a flag if a point in the path is missed or behind schedule. These periodic reports can often point out potential trouble before it becomes actual trouble. (CPM is discussed at length in Section 10.)

New-Product Testing

The determination of the takeover point where responsibility for quality shifts from research and development to manufacturing can be programmed as part of CPM. Usually, research and development or quality engineering develops specifications and tests for each new product. If this is done carefully and thoughtfully, the takeover by manufacturing can be made smoothly at the start of production. Quality control must be included in all planning and discussions to assure that the specifications are suitable, that methodology is compatible with existing or obtainable skills, and that suitable instrumentation is either available or obtainable. Some companies appoint a standing specifications committee composed of representatives from all groups involved in getting the product into production.

New Testing Equipment

It is evident that as the complexity of products increases, a parallel increase in the complexity of testing equipment is to be anticipated. In the electronics industry, for example, the ability to develop a complex product may be entirely negated if equipment sufficiently sensitive to test its reliability is not available or cannot be developed. The production of space hardware provides another example of this phenomenon. Requirements for environmental control in the aerospace industry have brought an entirely new approach. A professional group, the American Association for Contamination Control, accumulates and disseminates information on the methodology required to achieve and evaluate facilities which are not only free of particulate matter but are also biologically clean. This points up the fact that a company or an industry must meet increasing demands for sophisticated test equipment and production facilities in order to survive.

Improving Product Reliability

Early in the space program of the United States, an astronaut responded to a press inquiry about the state of his nerves before a space flight by asking the reporter how he would feel if he were about to orbit the earth in a machine consisting of several hundred thousand parts, each of which was made by the lowest bidder. The success of the space program is a monument to the ability to improve reliability to whatever degree the circumstances require.

Improving reliability depends on improvements in precision of measurement. Improved precision may, of course, be used to detect defects in the final product. However, its best application is the upgrading of in-process testing to prevent defects rather than detect them. Newly developed measurement devices with automatic readout, analysis, and feedback can check a critical operation minute by minute without waiting for many units to be produced, sampled, and tested. Almost instantaneous detection of an item which is "out-of-spec" often allows rapid correction so that the number of defective items produced is minimized.

Analyzing Quality Costs

Quality costs must be considered as a part of the overall company financial system. As such, they are an important consideration in planning the prevention system to produce defect-free products for the marketplace.

Engineering Function

Quality techniques, including those of statistical quality control, can be of great assistance in product planning. The objective of this planning is to develop a product that will function according to the requirements and that can also be produced without scrap, rework, or downtime. Many statistical quality control techniques (such as fractional or complete factorial designs) can be adapted to study the effect of changes in specifications or operating conditions on the quality of the product.

Inspection Labor and Equipment

The design of the product as it relates to its producibility exerts a major influence on the amount of quality control effort that must be expended to achieve success. A specification set tighter than necessary may strain production facilities and increase costs through added inspection. Surprisingly, it is often forgotten that tight specifications should be reserved for critical characteristics.

Scrap and Rework

It is essential to find the root causes for scrap and rework. The areas that should be searched include faulty design, unrealistic specifications, poor production methods, inadequate production equipment, and inadequate instruction of production personnel. Quality control must examine its own operation to be sure that it is not contributing by using an incorrect test method, inadequate sampling, or poor test equipment. All instrumentation, from the simplest gauge to the most complex electronic testing device, should be regularly checked (preferably against a standard material) to be sure that it is giving correct information. The maintenance of complete records on performance of test equipment is as important to quality as the records or production capability are to the production department. Ninety percent of the scrap and rework generated is usually a result of management's errors.

Defective Materials

Defective materials may not all originate with a vendor but may come from within the production complex. One department often produces a material or a part to be used by another unit within the same company. The problem of defective materials within a company involves the same considerations that apply to materials received from vendors. The classic solution to this problem, particularly if production is discontinuous, is to call on quality control to sample and test each part or material before the next production step. This is not the best solution; the necessity for it can be minimized or avoided by instituting meaningful prevention systems or in-process controls during production. In either case, strict attention to and complete understanding of specifications and test methods by both the producing and using departments are required.

Field Service

A company that services what it sells can find itself burdened with significant costs when it produces a defective product. Service repair or replacement during a warranty period can be costly. Whether this service is provided by the company or the dealer, its cost is an important factor in the overall profit picture. Consumer service organizations publish ratings of automobiles and television sets on the basis of their record for frequency and cost of repair. Since this type of information is now readily available to consumers, sales are being lost as a result of poor quality. One industry was criticized in the public press and before Congress for depending too fully on its customers for quality evaluation. Many other industries are falling prey to the same unthinkable tactics today. It is likely that government and consumer pressures to eliminate defects will increase, particularly where public health and safety are involved.

Cost of Quality

In order to determine the effects of the quality system, and to see improvement, it is necessary to establish an objective measurement, one that everyone can relate to. In the conventional quality systems, measurements are established around defect rates or indices of some type. What is needed is a measurement that can be readily communicated to a larger number of people. The measurement found most useful, especially in dealing with senior management, is the cost of quality. The cost of quality has two classifications: cost of conformance and cost of nonconformance.

The cost of conformance comprises those costs associated with preventing defects (design review, vendor approval, process controls, etc.) and appraising to determine if the requirements have been met (inspection, test, audit, vendor surveillance, etc.). The cost of nonconformance is made up of the costs related to failure, or not doing something right the first time (rework, scrap, redesign, reinspection, purchase order changes, returns, rebates, product liabilities, etc.) Unless these costs are identified, collected, and eliminated, a company could continue to waste as much as 20 to 25 percent of its sales dollar.

Through management of the cost of quality, it becomes apparent where to concentrate resources to receive the greatest gains. By systematic elimination of failure costs through implementation of prevention techniques a company can realize a handsome increase in profit dollars.

In order for this system to work, it is essential that the cost of quality be meticulously organized, accurate, and timely. It is also important that each element (scrap, rework, design review, audit, etc.) be traceable to a source. Only in this fashion will correct determination be made for the establishment of prevention systems. Collection and identification of these costs should be nonpunitive; in other words, this report should not be used to locate areas needing disciplinary action, but instead should identify areas needing help.

The cost-of-quality report can be one of the most effective management tools, and if properly managed can make quality improvement a significant contributor to the company's profits.

Budget Compliance

Modern accounting procedures and long-range forward planning require a realistic forecast of operating expenses and capital requirements for each operating unit. Yearly budgets are required as long as six months in advance of the start of the year, and management often needs a realistic forecast as far as five years ahead. Each significant variance must be explained. Examination of the reason for variance can aid in generating realistic forecasts of future operations. One usual cause of variance is overtime. This may result from increased workload, insufficient staffing, or the necessity to meet production schedules. Overtime may indicate decreased efficiency in quality control; this can be determined only if a realistic method of measuring output per man-hour can be established. The methods used by industrial engineering to set work standards and evaluate performance can be applied to quality control.

Improving Quality Performance

The quality achievement of a company depends on the attention given at all levels of management to short- and long-range planning for quality. If quality is recognized as a prime company objective, with constant involvement by all of management and with the responsibilities for quality input clearly defined, the quality goal can be reached.

Personnel motivation. Effective upgrading of the abilities and dedication of people is another important facet of the search for quality improvement. The dedication to quality improvement must be from the top down. If the boss can demonstrate his involvement in improving quality, he can involve others. If he gives only lip service, he cannot expect others to do more. "Zero defects" programs have been highly successful only where there was demonstrable involvement by top management. Dismal failure occurs when this involvement is absent.

Management responsibility. The achievement of quality is a management responsibility, and all systems of product planning, facilities design, and data feedback must be keyed to achieve a company's policy, which should be to make quality as important as cost and schedule.

The quality image can be promoted and communicated to the public by the company's public relations department or as part of its institutional advertising program. It is a serious mistake to promote a quality image unless it can be backed by quality performance. Lack of quality will result in loss of market share and ultimate demise.

□ *Jay W. Leek* (and *Roderick S. Cowles,* the original
author of this now substantially revised section)

MAINTENANCE MANAGEMENT

As manufacturing processes in all industries have been modernized by automation, higher speeds, large single-train operations, and electronic controls, the man-hours of productive labor per pound or piece (or any unit) have decreased, while the size of the maintenance force has necessarily increased to maintain the additional machinery. This trend will continue. The emergence of maintenance as a larger item on the cost sheet and thus a greater factor in profitability brings maintenance into focus as a major force in the success or failure of a business. It is imperative that today's maintenance effort be directed by modern managers using modern methods.

The goal of good maintenance management is to achieve optimum maintenance level at minimum cost in a safe manner. Optimum maintenance is that level of maintenance which permits the unit to produce in quantities and at quality required by sales demands.

Creating an Effective Organization

The top maintenance position—manager, superintendent, chief, by whatever title—should have equal rank with the top production job. (Production people are usually not maintenance-oriented and are unable to manage for maximum service at minimum cost.) Lower ranking or submergence in the operating organization is not recommended. It must not be inferred, however, that maintenance should become a separate empire, since it is strictly a service function. Rather, the top production man and the top maintenance man should display the ultimate in cooperation while dealing with each other as equals. A company is fortunate if it has a top maintenance man who has had production experience or at least has a good "feel" for production problems. Extensive previous maintenance experience up through the line is probably not necessary; it may even be a detriment. Today's maintenance demands a fresh, new look unhampered by "the way we have done it in the past."

It is recommended, first, that the top person have an engineering background; the particular discipline is not important, as there are many successful managers from mechanical, civil, electrical, and chemical engineering disciplines.

Second, he must be a leader, since the maintenance effort is not particularly adaptable to the driving technique. The maintenance manager does not make repairs himself; the output of the department is the result of his working with and through people.

The good manager needs one or two subordinates who have potential for the manager's job and whom he is training. Such men might appear on the organization chart as assistant manager, general foreman, planning supervisor, plant engineer, or other. The surest way to promotion is to have a replacement trained and ready. Middle levels of maintenance management are not discussed in detail here, since the number of levels and number of people vary widely. In most cases, the managers of tomorrow will come from these middle levels; thus the middle level of today should include the type of person, with appropriate background, that is needed in the manager's position.

The first-line foreman is, perhaps, the forgotten man in the maintenance organization. He bears the brunt of union push-pull activity while being pressured from above by his superior for greater productivity and lower costs. He deserves more attention. Many first-line foremen are promoted craftsmen and still retain the ideas and prejudices they had as hourly workers.

It is strongly recommended that, when promotion is from the hourly-rated group, psychological testing be used to supplement performance records and foreman recommendations. While not cheap, the cost for testing is miniscule compared with the money a poor foreman can waste. A new foreman should be given opportunity to take management development courses, encouraged to read books germane to his field, and offered opportunity to further his education with tuition assistance (if possible), since most first-line foremen do not have the educational background to permit much advancement in today's maintenance organizations.

An effective maintenance organization needs the related departments that will make it effective: planning and scheduling, plant engineering, and maintenance storeroom. An extremely useful adjunct is industrial engineering, but this group would more logically report to the plant or works manager.

Appraising the Existing Organization

Appraising an organization is most effectively done by evaluating results rather than studying organization charts, procedures, and people to see if they conform with modern management theories. The chief function of all levels of management is to produce profits or contribute to profits.

By definition, to measure is to compare with a standard; with maintenance, the difficult problem is to find the standard. A number of indices can be used; some are absolute and factual, and others are indicators only. The first comparison is total maintenance expenditures: this year versus last year; this month versus last month; comparison of total costs over, say, a ten-year period. While widely used, these comparisons are of doubtful real value because they give no effect to important variables such as production level or changing wage rates. A better yardstick is cost per unit of production expressed as dollars or percentage of total unit cost. This type of evaluation gets into the profit statement, since total profit is the product of unit profit and volume.

The comparison of maintenance costs per unit on a calendar basis gives the maintenance manager and his superiors a powerful tool to determine maintenance contributions to increased or deteriorated profits. A favorable trend whets management's appetite for more; unfavorable results demand corrective action. If action is indicated there are several areas to probe.

1. Wage rates are continuously increasing in all areas of operation; therefore, increases in maintenance rates should not have too great an impact, particularly on a percentage basis.
2. An increase in maintenance hours per unit of production means a possible decrease in maintenance labor efficiency.
3. An increase in the labor-to-material ratio is another indicator of decreased labor efficiency.
4. A sharp increase in maintenance material, both per unit of production and total, may indicate the need for replacement of old equipment. The cause must be determined.
5. An increase in emergencies and overtime orders indicates reversion to breakdown maintenance or insufficiently controlled operations.

The probe areas are symptoms that merit continuing attention to possibly fore-stall unfavorable maintenance costs. Many other comparisons, such as mainte-nance as a percentage of fixed capital, can be used; but their validity must be checked for the individual situation.

Planning and Scheduling

Maintenance may be classified as *breakdown* or *planned,* with many gradations be-tween the two. Few companies run on a strictly breakdown basis because of the high cost and limitation on production. Most organizations use at least rudimen-tary planning and scheduling. Conversely, there are few companies that could not profitably improve or enlarge their planning and scheduling effort.

Objectives

Planning and scheduling contributes to the goal of achieving optimum mainte-nance at minimum cost by decreasing machine downtime, utilizing manpower more effectively, adjusting workforce to demand, planning for major jobs, and anticipating repetitive jobs.

Work Order Systems

A work order system is the first step in setting up planning and scheduling. Work orders may be simple or complex, but the simplest form that will fulfill the local needs is probably the best. As a bare minimum, the following information must be included: description of work requested; location; urgency or priority; name and code number of department for charging; signature of originator and space for approvals if required; a number for identification and collection of charges. As an organization becomes more sophisticated, more data can be in-cluded to permit processing and analyzing by EDP.

With a work order system, it is possible to take the first step from breakdown maintenance toward planned maintenance by preparing daily work schedules, one day at a time. The effect should be apparent immediately, since each crafts-man will know at the start of a workday where he is expected to be and what ma-chine he is to work on. Work schedules, even the most simple, are a strong force toward real maintenance management. At this point, it should be emphasized that work schedules, whether crude or sophisticated, will always be broken to handle true emergencies.

A weekly schedule is recommended after some experience with daily sched-ules. This is prepared at a joint meeting with operating supervision. A further logical extension is the monthly schedule, handled in much the same manner as the weekly—by conference with production supervision. In the daily schedule, practically all the workforce will be committed (scheduled). The weekly schedule might commit 75 percent to 80 percent of the force, and the monthly no more than 50 percent. This is done to permit orderly scheduling of unanticipated work. The longer-term schedules permit the scheduling of preventive mainte-nance and repetitive jobs which might be overlooked in day-to-day scheduling.

Short-Term and Long-Term Planning

A logical extension of work orders and scheduling is planning, both long- and short-term. A schedule must make at least a rough estimate of the time required for a job, but estimates of this type are usually too liberal. The planner is expected to make a more realistic time estimate. In addition, there is the problem of materials: Are they available, or must they be purchased? Where more than one craft is involved, the job needs to be sequenced. Production should be consulted on how the job would fit in with production schedules. With a planner in the picture, the scheduler receives a "package" instead of a bare work order. Savings in time resulting from having the necessary materials on hand or even delivered to the job site will often justify the salary of a planner. Closer estimates of time required and sequencing in a multicraft situation allow the scheduler to prepare more meaningful schedules.

Longer-range planning on weekly, monthly, and annual bases follow in logical order. The problem of necessary materials, spare parts, and the like is of great importance in longer-range planning. Since some parts call for deliveries up to one year apart, the position of a job on the long-range schedule is often dictated by their delivery date. Long-range planning also provides an opportunity for leveling manpower. It is also a vehicle for noting, for example, the annual state inspection of boilers and the annual (or less frequent) inspection of machinery. Once on a long-range plan, items recorded will not be overlooked; furthermore, such records help fill the gap when key people leave the organization through promotion, transfer, or another reason.

Manpower Requirements

On a daily basis, the scheduler can schedule only the man-hours that he knows he will have available for the next day. The same principle applies to weekly and monthly schedules; however, with these longer-period plans it becomes possible to start leveling manpower.

Work order priorities.   Many priority systems are available, some very complex. A simple system of four priorities will suffice in many situations: (1) emergency (do now, no scheduling); (2) urgent (do within 24 hours, scheduled but not planned); (3) schedule (as implied—planned and scheduled); and (4) shutdown (as implied).

On a daily basis, the scheduler first schedules his urgent orders and then fills out available manpower with schedule orders.

Backlog.   A symptom of shortage of manpower, owing either to actual lack of hands or to poor utilization, is a gradual buildup of schedule orders. This backlog is the most potent indicator available for adjusting the workforce. Conversely, a decrease in backlog is an invitation to reduce the force. Short-term changes in backlog have little significance, but longer-term trends—say, several weeks or a month—definitely require action. If a rising backlog is noted but thought owing to poor manpower utilization, it may still be necessary to temporarily increase the workforce, since the improvement of manpower utilization and worker efficiency cannot be accomplished quickly. Again, maintenance is a service department and the machines must be kept running.

Timekeeping Program

Timekeeping serves two purposes: The worker must be paid for the hours he works, and the time he spends on a job must be charged to the proper department or cost center (in some systems, to the individual machine). The first is usually recorded on an individual weekly time card by a punch-type time clock. The question of charging the worker's time to the right "customer" is more complex. A clerk-type timekeeper is sometimes used; he circulates through the plant, noting jobs being worked on and time chargeable. This is not an efficient practice. With a work order system, the foreman may keep the time by noting the hours on the work order before he turns it in as completed. This system works very well, and there is only one possible objection: It makes paperwork for the foreman. A third system being adopted in many plants is to have the worker note his own time on the work order. Bear in mind that the worker is being paid according to the record on his time card. He has nothing to gain from a false entry on the work order. If there is a problem of low productivity, it must be solved by other means than the distribution of his daily time to job orders. Further, in the normal industrial organization there is little to be gained from accuracy to the minute in charging time to a work order.

Scheduled and Unscheduled Shutdowns

An unscheduled shutdown is usually an emergency. As such, the normal daily schedule is broken to provide the necessary manpower. Even in this emergency situation, the planner and the scheduler can be of invaluable assistance. The scheduler can pull manpower from noncritical jobs in other areas to make up the required force. The planner, from prior knowledge of the area, can locate necessary parts and get them delivered; he can dispatch special apparatus such as welding machines, burning outfits, impact wrenches, and portable air compressors; he can alert the machine shop for any special parts to be made or repaired. Companies that have a well-organized planning and scheduling function will attest that unscheduled or emergency shutdowns are definitely shortened by its efforts even though the job obviously could not be planned and scheduled in the usual manner.

Planned shutdowns are one of the shining areas where planning and scheduling really pay off. In a well-structured situation, the planner would be accumulating individual work orders (priority-shutdown) as the production people see the need. These work orders would be individually processed, labor estimated, material availability checked (or ordered), and special tools noted. When the shutdown is scheduled, the planner and scheduler assemble the pertinent work orders and may plot out a bar graph or even prepare a critical path chart. This furnishes the necessary data for manning. The savings possible with this method —both in dollars and time—over a nonplanned, hit-or-miss style are tremendous.

Materials and Labor Cost Controls

Controls over labor, materials, and overhead are necessary if maintenance is to make its contribution to profitability and profit improvement. True costs, by areas or departments, must be known in order to control them. The work order system will allocate direct labor to the proper cost center. A system must also be devised to charge materials to the proper user.

Materials and Inventory Control

All maintenance organizations have some sort of storeroom. Apart from raw materials, 80 percent or more of the storeroom is used specifically for maintenance. The storeroom exists for the purpose of having on tap the repair parts and materials that may be required to minimize machine downtime. On long-delivery spare parts where lead time can be up to a year or more, there is no alternative but to have an adequate supply on hand. A typical store may have items with individual values from a few cents to $100,000. Stores management has undergone changes in recent years. Several areas that contribute to decreased total stores inventory while maintaining adequate supplies to expedite maintenance are as follows:

Decontrol of low-cost items. Many companies no longer require requisitions for these items ($1 limit), which are charged to overhead when received and are placed in free-access bins. A few companies have raised the limit to $2. Minor losses in these items have been found to be far less than the accounting expense for processing requisitions.

The ABC system of inventory control. This takes into account both the cost of possession and the cost of acquisition. It concentrates stores and purchasing effort on the high-cost items. Considerable economies can be achieved under this system.

The stockless storeroom. This is chiefly applicable in populous areas. A supplier of bearings, for example, agrees to hold in his stock a certain number, size, and type of bearings for the customer. This is covered by a blanket order. He will ship any designated bearing by release against this blanket order, using his own truck, common carrier, or taxicab, depending upon urgency.

Requisitions. Normally, a stores requisition is required for any item taken from stores. This requisition should show the work order number. The use of the work order number ties together material and labor on a job for later evaluation and application to the proper cost center. The stores area should be enclosed, with limited access, and in general out of bounds except to stores employees.

Quantities. Quantities of any item carried are a function of usage and lead time for replacement. Many plants function with a perpetual inventory system, using a maximum-minimum setup or reorder point in case of ABC. In order for this to function, there must be a feedback from the requisition; a card system is often used with clerks posting withdrawals and pulling a card for purchasing when minimum or reorder point is reached. This function is also compatible with EDP. Additionally, an inventory check system (continuous or cyclical) is needed where one-twelfth of the stock is inventoried each month. On a maximum-minimum setup, the limits should be constantly reviewed to see if they can be decreased—again, aiming at decrease in total inventory. A good rule of thumb is that inventory (dollar value) should turn over once every three to six months (for chemical plants, once every one or two years is considered more reasonable). Periodic reviews should be made of slow-moving items showing no transaction in one to three years, depending upon the industry, to see if they cannot be removed from inventory and put on an on-request basis.

Carrying charge. The cost of stores inventory is considerable. In one plant, it has been estimated as 23 percent of the value of the inventory per year; higher costs have been used but they are unusual. It is made up of such items as the cost of capital; local and state personal property taxes; salaries of personnel; cost of warehouse facilities; and inventory insurance, theft, damage, and obsolescence.

Labor Standards

Standards systems and controls for labor are necessary to secure optimum maintenance at minimum cost. A work order system is mandatory for any program of labor standards.

Historical standards. Relatively simple to install, historical standards are widely used. The method consists of accumulating the labor hours for repetitive jobs, starting at any point in time. Each repetitive job is recorded on a separate sheet of multicolumn paper. As the job is repeated, an entry shows the date, the hours required, and any special conditions. After a few entries, an average is taken for all normal occurrences; this becomes the standard time to be allotted by the planner. Average or standard is updated from time to time. If on any job the time is found in excess of standard, questions can be asked, thus furnishing a measure of control. If improvements are made in planning, scheduling, materials delivery, supervision, or other areas, they quickly show up by "beating the standard," thus providing a measure of the effectiveness of the improvements. There is much to be said in favor of historical standards. Their principal disadvantage is that they are comparative rather than absolute. In other words, a company's performance might be so bad that even a considerable improvement as measured by historical standards might leave it far below an acceptable level.

Engineered work standards. Engineered work standards apply a standard time to a job. Most consultants have a system of engineered work standards that they generally recommend. A standards book is supplied that contains tables for various mechanical acts. In developing a standard time for a particular job, the planner breaks it down into its smallest components, looks up the standard time for each, and adds up the segments; this becomes the standard time. Though this process may appear to be excessively time-consuming, it need be done only once for each job. Standards so obtained are realistic in that the job can be accomplished in the stipulated time by a good mechanic.

In practice, the actual time is generally greater; figures of 60 percent to 80 percent efficiency are common. Furthermore, in most plants no more than 80 percent of the work orders are susceptible to engineered standards. The engineered standard does, however, provide a solid baseline against which performance can be measured. As with historical standards, improvements in techniques are readily apparent in increased percentage efficiency.

Improved scheduling. Use of standards is bound to improve performance by permitting tighter scheduling. In the absence of standards, the planner is usually too liberal in the time allowed, with the result that the worker either uses Parkinson's law ("The job expands to fill the time allowed") or is idle. Standards plus improved or tighter scheduling will result in lower labor costs and better manpower planning.

Budgets

Maintenance may range from 5 percent to 15 percent of total production costs; thus it swings considerable weight in cost-profitability studies. The budget must be tight enough to contribute to profitability yet be attainable. In most plants, the new budget leans heavily on previous years' experience, particularly the current year's. In its simplest form, the new budget is the current year's experience adjusted to compensate for increased wage rates, known major repairs, improvements in efficiency, and level of operations. The attempt should be made to identify as many jobs as possible for the coming year, both for cost and timing. Identification of major portions of the budget money as separate, discrete jobs is of great assistance in manpower leveling. It also permits a greater degree of control. Preventive maintenance may be shown as a separate budget item.

The first yardstick used to appraise the maintenance effort is usually budget compliance for both labor and materials. Although this comparison used in a vacuum is not a particularly valid measuring device, it is the way maintenance costs appear on the cost sheet and bears directly on the cost-profitability picture. Obviously, materials and labor for individual jobs should be continuously compared with the estimate, and tabulations prepared on a weekly, monthly, and annual basis. EDP is of great assistance in this effort.

Improving and Appraising Maintenance Performance

Improved maintenance performance is not confined to costs; it is equally important to increased operating time on machines, modifications to increase output, and decreased operating labor. These items may actually increase overall maintenance expenditures but will pay off in increasd productivity.

Preventive Maintenance Program

Preventive maintenance is practiced to some extent in every organization; it is a potent contributor to profitability. In its simplest form, it might be defined as "detecting and repairing a fault in a machine before it actually breaks down." There is a popular belief that a PM program will reduce maintenance costs. This is not true, in most cases. A PM program will pay off chiefly in increased availability of machines, leading to more production and attendant benefits: improved scheduling of workers, better utilization of workforce, and possible elimination of major equipment repairs.

Equipment. A PM program can be started on any scale and applied to even one piece that may be troublesome but is vitally important to an operation. Even with an elaborate program, not all equipment is covered. If a company goes into a program on a piecemeal basis, equipment will be added to the PM list as pieces are identified as production deterrents.

Schedule. The PM program normally consists of four parts: lubrication, inspection, adjustment, and repairs. A schedule is set up for frequency, based on lubrication requirements and known or estimated frequency of repair. The PM inspector handles the first three items, noting repairs needed, and the repairs are scheduled in the normal manner according to urgency, machine availability, and manpower. Records can be simple or elaborate. A master PM schedule is necessary for the schedules so that they can set up the PM work on the appropriate day. One way of handling work orders is a yearly PM order for each cost center. EDP can be used to good advantage in developing schedules.

Cost allocation. The allocation of cost is not difficult for an organization that has a work order system plus planning and scheduling. The costs for PM would go to the proper cost center, and the actual repairs would also be charged properly by the regular work order.

Evaluation. Evaluating the results of a PM program is often difficult. The availability of a machine or process and the frequency of breakdowns or emergency shutdowns can be compared with previous conditions; improvements in each of these categories might be expected. Total maintenance costs also should be evaluated, although little or no improvement may be noted. In any event, total maintenance costs are an unreliable yardstick for maintenance effectiveness. Maintenance on a unit basis—cost per unit of production—should show improvement after the program has been implemented.

Developing Performance Data

Meaningful performance data should be developed so that improvements can be evaluated qualitatively and, hopefully, quantitatively. The simplest comparison (total maintenance this year or month against the same period last year) is of little real value; many other variables may be working to cloud the issue. A more accurate measure is the comparison of actual against standard time by job or of maintenance costs per unit of production for various periods. A significant decrease in this unit cost, for example, is honest added profit and a measure of effectiveness.

Worker efficiency. If work sampling is used, the performance index will show improvement, particularly as a result of planning and scheduling. The difference in the index before and after the installation of modern methods is often startling. The labor-to-materials ratio is another tool; a decrease in this ratio generally indicates improved manpower utilization. A decrease in emergency orders is a measure of PM effectiveness. A decrease in the backlog of work orders indicates improved maintenance efficiency. Although no single measure of work efficiency exists, these several tests should add up to a valid picture of trend.

Adherence to budget. Budget compliance is an unreliable tool to use in measuring a department or a manager, particularly on a month-to-month basis. A budget overrun is not necessarily bad, nor is an underrun always good. The evaluation of a monthly cost sheet to determine true position requires considerable study; mere comparison of budget against actual cost is of little value. The actual cost must be corrected for jobs canceled, jobs postponed, jobs done early, and unbudgeted jobs in order to arrive at a true position for an individual month. In such a comparison, it is a great advantage to have as large a portion of the budget as possible in identified jobs.

Timely job completion. Timely job completion is principally a function of the planning and scheduling effort. Very often, production runs are scheduled on the basis of the completion of a maintenance job, and considerable dollar losses can accrue if a job runs over. Maintenance promises on job completion and the production statement of the date required must be realistic, since chaos results if each group applies its own liberal safety factor.

Training. Increasing complexity of machinery, rapid technological change, increased size and speed of machines, and new construction materials all dictate that the knowledge and skills of the maintenance section be continuously updated. This means the training of all levels in new methods and techniques, plus additional education for supervisory levels through night classes, college extension courses, or other means. Many forces are at work to make training ever more important: technological change, early retirement, greater mobility of people, the expansion and addition of new facilities, and more.

For reference in training programs for salaried employees, the use of a replacement table is suggested. Such a table indicates replacements for all levels on the organization chart and contains columns for "years to get ready" and "training required." Adherence to the training recommendations will be of great help. An adjunct is a chart showing supervision, age, general estimate of health, any known data on early retirement, plans to move, and the like.

The old apprentice programs for hourly personnel appear to be losing favor; some of the newer techniques—programmed instruction, for example—might be used with young, intelligent new hires to develop them into good mechanics.

Staff requirements. A review of the staff should also be done periodically, asking such questions as: Is the type of organization adequate for the future? Has it been compromised to hide incompetents? Do authority and communication flow in short, straight lines? The answers to these and other questions will indicate the changes necessary to meet the future head on. Only the maintenance manager can make this study.

These several suggestions could result in a sound plan for the future. If the plan is sound, it must be implemented to be of value and cannot be compromised for expediency. □ **Gordon A. Coleman**

MANUFACTURING MANAGEMENT INFORMATION SYSTEMS

To be effective, manufacturing management information systems (MMIS) must provide appropriate information to *all* levels of the manufacturing organization. At the first level, the system must be capable of processing each transaction and supplying up-to-date status information to support operating personnel, first-line supervision, and lower-level managers in all production and production support areas in the factory and office for day-to-day operations. Figure 4-18 shows the functional relationships and how they extend through the entire organization. This first level, the foundation of the entire system, must encompass the controlled inputs from all activities—the storage and processing of the data to provide accurate and timely information on the movement, status, and value of all materials, labor, facilities, and paperwork related to shipping and production requirements and availabilities.

At the second level, the system must perform analyses based on the latest status and plan information for possible planning and rescheduling decisions by middle managers.

At the third level, the system should provide middle and upper management with the means for planning and control decision making by (1) evaluating both past and projected performance, (2) simulating effects of alternative possible plans on a "what if" basis, and (3) responding to special information requests.

The controlled input of the MMIS first level is critical. Adequate organizational responsibilities, secured storage facilities, manual procedures, and disciplines must be specified and implemented for physical material and paperwork control. This fundamental step should be completed and proved before use of the data at the second or third levels. Full integration with management accounting at the very beginning of the systems development greatly assists in this area to simultaneously achieve the first-level goals and greater cost benefits.

Companies are ill-advised to proceed into the second level simultaneously with the first. The lure of current materials management systems which include comparison reports to evaluate availability against requirements for individual parts and assemblies, revised schedules, or priorities, etc. should not tempt manufacturing managers to enter this level too early. Such reports are meaningless until the procedures and data at the first level are corrected. Otherwise the materials management groups will find themselves unable to handle the paperwork load generated by the system. Production and other work in the department would be affected. Hot lists and expediting would thrive.

At the third level, there has been a serious neglect in MMIS development. Early efforts concentrated on data base management and processing internal to the computer. Later, more attention was given to the information and report formats required in materials management and data collection operations. Today, many workable software application packages are available for these areas. Distributed data processing using minicomputers can be a more beneficial mode of operation. Made feasible by greatly reduced cost of computer hardware with built-in data base management systems and so-called friendly interactive software application packages for use by people who are not computer specialists, distributed data processing permits a large portion of the processing of detail data to be located at the operating site. Tie-in is maintained with central data processing but fewer data are transmitted, thus reducing total cost. Total responsibility for the MMIS operation is located at the manufacturing site. Processing turnaround times are reduced, and flexibility for scheduling regular processing or doing special jobs is increased.

Figure 4-18. Typical manufacturing management information system—functional flow.

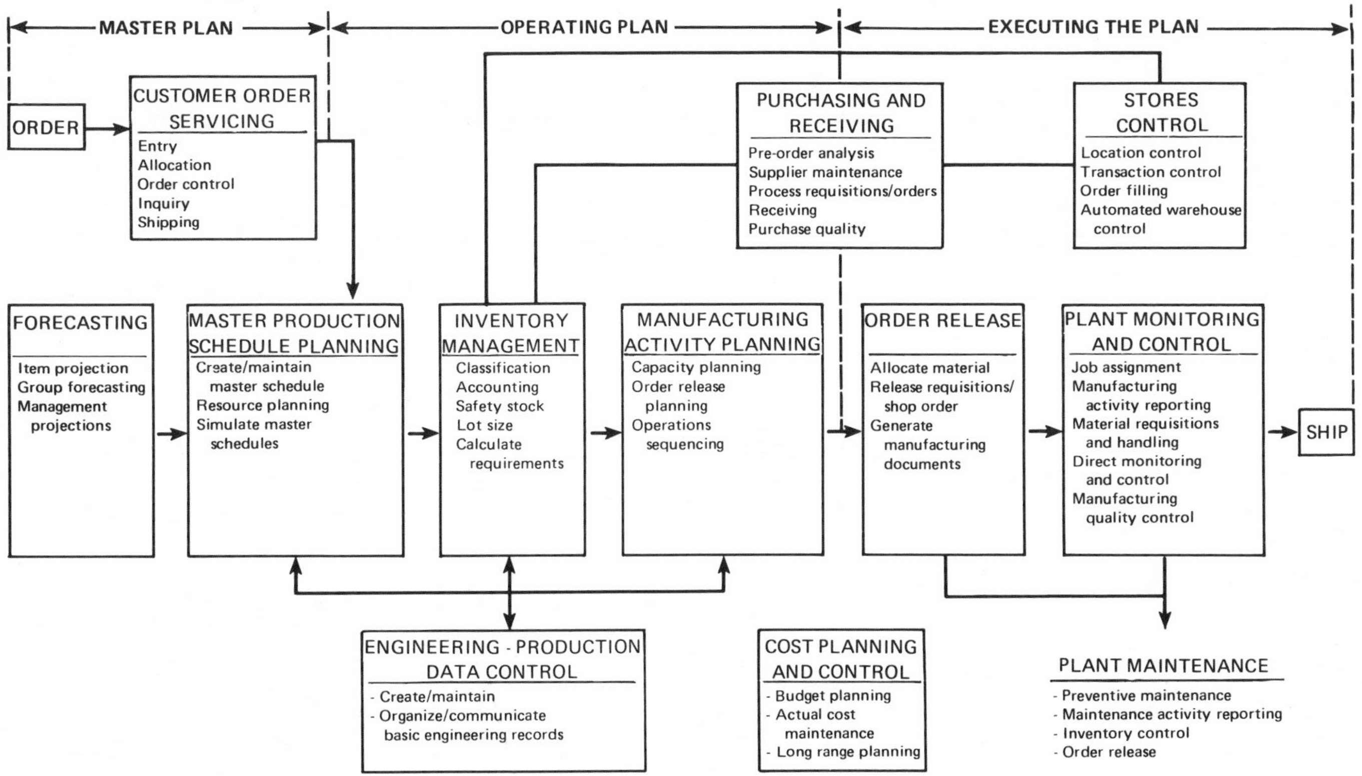

Performance Management

To satisfy upper- and middle-management requirements, there should be full integration of MMIS and management accounting for detail accuracy and interdepartment accountability control. Simplified charts or reports are needed to provide management *visibility* for control of (1) timely and accurate performance of key production support functions from sales through stores material issue to production, (2) timely performance of vendors and production areas, particularly those making the basic parts and subassemblies, and (3) performance results from the MMIS and the manufacturing team covering pure financial and related goals of inventory, on-time shipments, expediting, and so forth. Also needed are integrated portrayals for upper-management decision making—for example, an assimilation of the latest data relating to sales forecasts, inventories, on-order availabilities, expected production output, and vendor inputs to project total performance levels and measure accountabilities.

What is required to satisfy these needs is merely a focusing of attention and a reassessment of information, not new data processing hardware or concepts. Basic data are already captured by the system in most cases but such data must be organized and presented in brief understandable form to become useful information. For example, monthly data reports for the last two fiscal years might be summarized into one sheet of pertinent information. Exception reports, charts, and graphs all help to serve this purpose.

To be most useful, the information must be timely, selective, and comprehensive to provide the earliest possible warning of *potential* problems and give maximum time for corrective action. Current *and* projected schedule performance information for preproduction and production support functions affecting *future* production and shipments is much more useful and effective in maintaining on-time deliveries than information regarding the shortages still delaying yesterday's scheduled deliveries.

Management Visibility Control

In some cases, simplified and less precise but more meaningful units of measure can be utilized for comprehension by all levels in the organization and for ease of upper-management controls. One example is useful to company presidents, heads of manufacturing, managers, and first-line supervision.

Management visibility control is a simple method of visual communication for rapid quantitative performance evaluation. Its purpose is effective planning and control by management, supervision, and employees. It is equally beneficial to companies with computerized or manual control systems. Because of its simplicity and negligible cost, it is effective in small as well as large companies.

It is applied to strategic support functions, as well as to production areas, permitting early identification of potential problems while there is time to work on solutions. It greatly enhances production flow, motivating and coordinating supervision, shortening lead times, and improving productivity, inventory turnover, and on-time delivery performance. It speeds up implementation of MRP systems. In companies not getting results expected from existing systems, it pinpoints problem areas and guides management to make the system operative. It stimulates schedule and reporting disciplines required to maintain the accurate data base essential to the successful operation of all systems.

In this system, appropriate strategic control points (Figure 4-19) are selected, and the applicable tally counts and charts (Figures 4-20, 4-21, and 4-22) are used to create a managerial control that communicates to all levels of the organization. Management visibility control can be used to advantage in any of the following operations: (1) plants with problems of frequent schedule changes or production delays, materials shortages, late shipments, high work-in-process inventory, long lead times, or low productivity; (2) plants that must rely on heavy expediting or long production coordination meetings to keep production and shipments flowing; (3) plants with materials requirements planning or other materials control systems that have not yet produced expected improvements; (4) plants planning or implementing new systems; and (5) accounting, purchasing, engineering, materials control, customer order processing, receiving, stores, shop areas, packing, shipping, and other departments responsible for regular processing of paperwork or physical materials.

Management visibility control can generate major cost reductions because it does the following:

□ Motivates and helps supervisors and managers to work together to correct common operating problems that cause delays and inefficiencies.
□ Provides easy visibility of performance in production and office areas for quantitative evaluation.
□ Gives early warning where action is required to avoid production interruptions and maintain shipping schedules.
□ Provides first-line supervision with an effective communications channel for problem resolution and prevention.
□ Distinguishes responsibility for production *support* functions from production functions.
□ Maintains performance accountability.
□ Illustrates where and how existing production management and materials control systems can be made more effective.
□ Provides a simple effective means of developing adherence to operating and reporting procedures and to maintaining a more accurate data base.
□ Clearly defines expected performance by first-line supervisors and triggers action on chronic problems out of their area of control.
□ Measures performance on the basis of the number of *documents*, a unit to which each department is already accustomed. Examples include purchase requisitions, shop orders, and engineering releases. Produces immediate results upon implementation in the first functional area. Within three months after all key areas start using the technique, the following benefits become apparent: less expediting and more on-time shipments, fewer production delays and higher productivity, and shorter shop lead times and lower inventory.

Figure 4-19. Management visibility control—typical strategic control points.

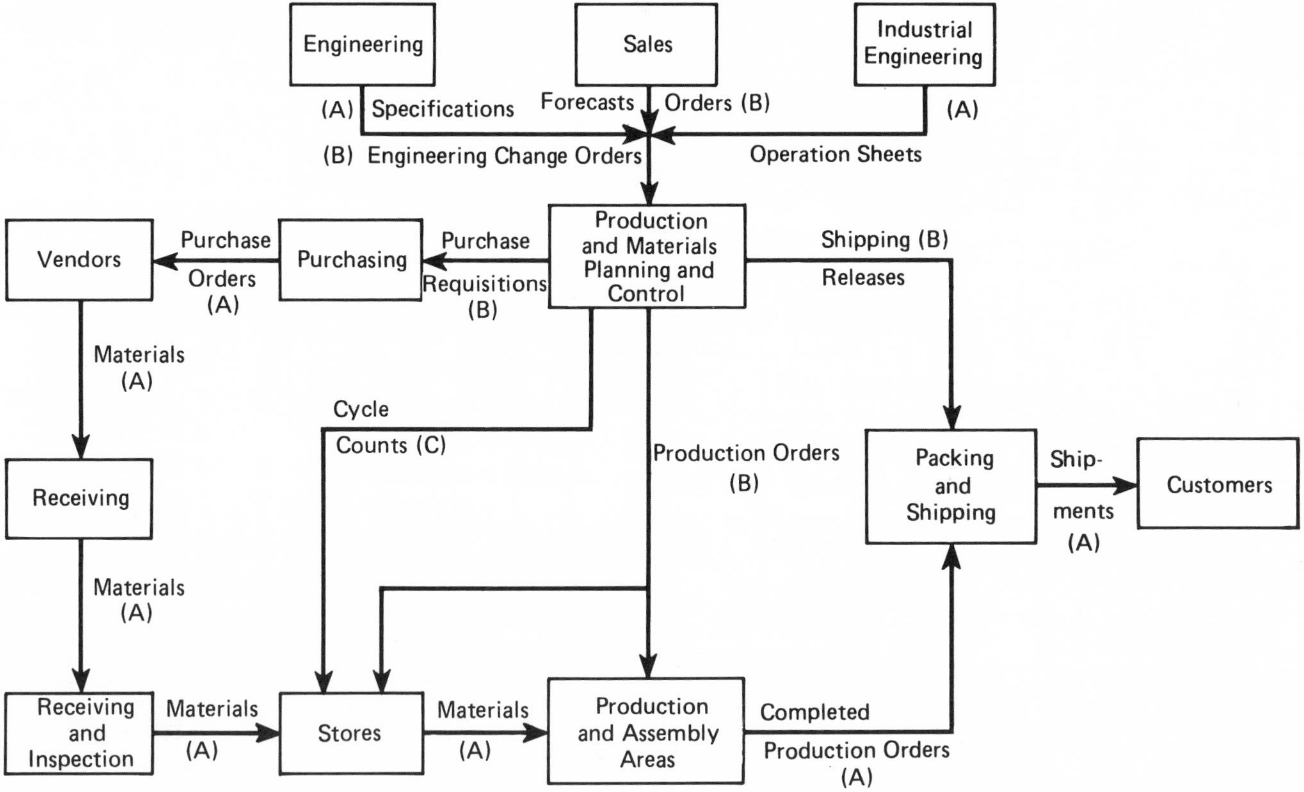

Figure 4-20. Sample chart (A): shop loading and schedule performance control, machine shop.

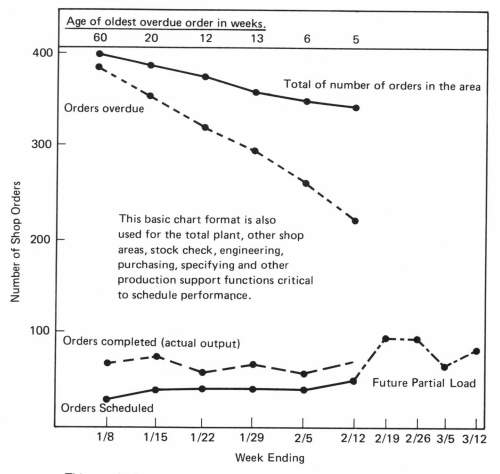

This sample shows:

1. A potential increase in contract overdues 8–10 weeks from now resulting from the additional shortages on the assembly areas that will be generated by this department.
2. An average lead time of 2.5 weeks greater than normal.
3. Steady reduction in the total number of overdue orders.
4. Steady reduction in the age of the oldest overdue from 60 weeks to 5.
5. Future partial load greater than current output.
6. Possibility that scheduling and loading have not been considering capacity.
7. Potential increase in overdue orders unless action is taken to increase capacity or reschedule load.
8. Possibility that the order mix has changed and completed orders should increase, and overdues continue to decrease.

Figure 4-21. Sample chart (B): work order, or purchase requisition control weekly activity report.

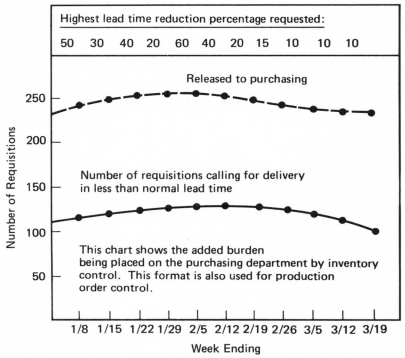

Measuring Results

To make MMIS effective, results must be measured in a discerning manner. Conventional overall financial results tell only the final chapter and may perpetuate causes of poor results. As an unbiased management control function, management accounting performs a valuable service in this regard. Disciplining the single forecast is an excellent example. Delineation of responsibility for performances makes a major contribution for improved operating results. Beyond the conventional financial measures, however, MMIS must be measured against certain key operating conditions and absolutes. A successful MMIS must result in increased productivity, inventory turnover, and on-time shipments and reduced expediting.

To determine the system's effectiveness and communicate the importance of these results they must be measured continually against plan. It may be necessary to net out the effects from certain factors outside of manufacturing. If this is the

Figure 4-22. Sample chart (C): cycle count control.

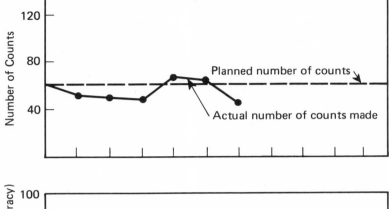

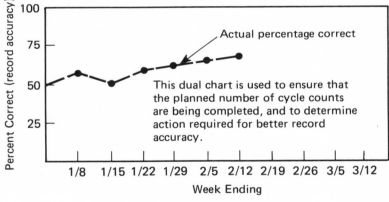

case, poor performance of the outside and/or manufacturing areas is likely to be corrected earlier when accountability is so delineated. Outside factors are often related to forecasts, actual customer demand, and their *timing* and mixes. The added dimensions of time and mix complicate the performance measurement. For example, a poor forecast, if reappraised early enough, may have no effect on manufacturing performance, whereas an accurate total forecast with wide variations in order input or mix may be very damaging.

Inventory Flow Analysis

Inventory performance also should be measured against an absolute standard for the particular manufacturing facility. Such a procedure identifies out-of-balance conditions to effect significant inventory reductions.

Inventory flow analysis is a highly effective approach to balancing and reducing inventories. It relates physical materials flow with time and cost to determine the proper production inventory investment and turnover for any plant or business. It provides an inventory management control for division presidents, finance officers, manufacturing vice presidents, and asset managers.

Very significant improvements in inventory investment and turnover are achieved quickly because (1) the approach motivates all participants, (2) the logic is simple and easily understood, (3) inventory targets are determined by the persons responsible for balancing and reducing the inventory, (4) the inventory and turnover targets for any given plant can be determined in one day or less, (5) proper inventory and turnover levels are determined on a realistic basis, and (6) the inventory targets are established consistent with accounting classification and valuation procedures for proper and easy performance measurement.

Planning and Execution

General management, manufacturing, marketing, engineering, and finance jointly develop the business plan for the coming year. Sales, inventory, and production levels are projected, and manufacturing is then held responsible for producing and shipping the products on time without incurring costs or inventories in excess of budgeted amounts.

At the time the business plan is developed, the production plan specifies the overall level of manufacturing output based on sales forecasts for product groupings or families of products. The specific products or items that must be produced and shipped are projected later on a continuing basis and within a shorter time frame, utilizing most recent customer order experience. It is vital that the aggregate and mix of these short-term product forecasts be correlated with the official planning forecast monthly to maintain one realistic sales forecast for universal use and acceptance as the common planning base for all sectors of the company. Proper planning of production, facilities, personnel, tooling, finance, and marketing cannot be maintained without this fundamental control except in those rare cases where actual orders are consistent with the initial forecast. Yet this vital control is frequently neglected and must be maintained by manufacturing to preclude disastrous over- or underproduction. Manufacturing's purpose in maintaining this control should not be to revise the forecast but rather to make sure that the proper personnel maintain a proper forecast from which manufacturing can develop a proper production and inventory plan.

Master production scheduling (MPS) and materials requirement planning (MRP) are used for planning and budget determination as well as day-to-day execution of the plan, coping with changes in customer order input, sales forecasts and production/vendor performances, or generating new replenishment orders and priorities required as time progresses. (See also the discussion on "Materials Management" in this section.)

Master Production Schedule

The MPS is a production schedule either for the products shipped or the stock components from which the final products shipped are customized or assembled to customer specifications. This schedule is made by comparing planned limitations and capabilities and on-hand inventories of each of the items to the actual and projected requirements to determine the quantities to be purchased or produced each week during the next year. Although forecast and accounting periods are generally calendar months or four- or five-week periods, the production scheduling period most commonly employed is one week.

Materials Requirement Planning System

Driven by the MPS, the MRP system is used to determine *when* and *what* materials are required from internal and external sources to satisfy the customer and inventory requirements of the MPS consistent with sales, production, inventory, quality, delivery, and financial plans and policies.

MRP is the successor to the reorder point (ROP) system. In the ROP system a minimum availability balance (reorder point) of on-hand plus on-order is maintained equal to a safety or reserve stock plus an average usage over the period of time (lead time) required to replenish the stock. Whenever a new requirement is posted bringing the available balance below the reorder point, an additional quantity is ordered for future requirements. This procedure must be repeated through all the parts to the lowest-level item in a multilevel assembly to order the items actually needed first. The process often takes weeks, and perceptive practitioners must develop circumventive methods to avoid the delays as much as possible.

ROP systems maintain an availability balance based on *average* total usage over lead time based on *historical* usage. No matter what forecasting method is used, the projected requirements are still based on past usage, and the available balance maintained is a resulting lump sum insensitive to the specific time of need.

MRP, on the other hand, projects requirements on a weekly basis far beyond manufacturing and procurement lead times by exploding the master production schedule for the top-level items through all levels of the bill of materials to the lowest-level part or material (see Figure 4-16). For each level item, the past-due and future requirements and the on-hand and on-order available balances for each week are maintained. A comparison of the two balances on a weekly accumulative basis identifies the need for reschedules and the specific time when additional quantities are required. Safety stock can be provided in advance of need for *realistic* quantities instead of average quantities, which are most frequently too much or too little.

All this would be of insufficient help, however, if it took as long as ROP to process through all levels. Even though MRP maintains appropriate balances for each item for each week a year into the future, the updating of status data and complete regeneration from the master production schedule can be accomplished overnight. This means that the effect of new sales forecasts, engineering changes, late vendor deliveries, etc. can be calculated within 24 hours, at most, eliminating the once most serious bottleneck in manufacturing operating systems. When planning functions and feedbacks from execution are joined with MRP the resulting system is called closed-loop MRP (see Figure 4-23).

MRP has been reviewed here thus far in terms of parts and materials planning,

Figure 4-23. Closed-loop MRP.

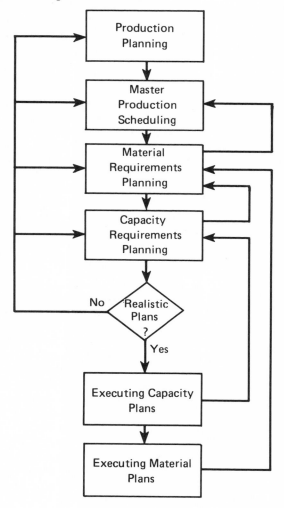

using a modified bill of materials containing parts and materials needed to make the higher-level assembly. When this type of structuring is applied to requirements for direct labor skill and time, or setup labor and time, indirect labor classification and time, machine time, space, energy, tooling, etc., any resource can be processed and planned with MRP. This expansion of MRP is called MRP II—manufacturing resource planning.

Since MRP is actually a simulation model, it can be used for answering "what if" questions and for long-range planning as well as for the short-range planning and execution described above. From the projection of personnel, facilities, and inventory, cash-flow requirements can be planned effectively.

Prerequisites for Success

Numerous manufacturing companies have adopted MRP quite successfully. The successful users of MRP are completely dedicated to the system and reap very high benefits. The unsuccessful users experience very high costs in personnel strain, added expediting and other personnel, low productivity, high inventory investment, and poor customer delivery. Unfortunately, respected authorities in computer hardware and software, management consulting, universities, and the American Production and Inventory Control Society (APICS) have found by actual survey that less than 10 percent of the MRP installations are successful.

An MRP system is successful only if it results in increased productivity, inventory turnover and on-time shipments, and reduced expediting. Too many so-called experts lose sight of the fact that the system's purpose is to produce tangible improvements in the business operation.

There are many proven MRP software packages available. Why, then, are there not many more successful MRP installations? The basic MRP software is not the problem. For an MRP system to be successful, virtually every person in finance, sales, engineering, manufacturing, quality control, purchasing, receiving, stores, materials handling, expediting, and even in the company management must follow some discipline or procedure relating to MRP.

Consider the following three requirements critical to the success of MRP system: (1) Master production schedules must be realistic. The total load must be within available capacity limits. Specific requirements must not be changed significantly beyond planned or feasible variations during the normal manufacturing and procurement lead times. This is commonly known as freezing the schedule through the prescribed period. (2) Bills of materials must be correct and up to date; they must coincide with the actual production or processing steps, both internal and external, particularly those corresponding to control points for the MRP and performance measurement systems. Conventional engineering and cost bills must be modified to meet these requirements. (3) Status data, particularly unfilled customer order requirements and on-hand and on-order balances, must be at least 95 percent accurate and up to date as of the common cutoff point used for all status data and the master production schedule.

For master production schedules to be realistic, forecasts must be realistic. Actual orders varying widely from forecasts in either direction attest to the lack of realism of the production schedules. Sales must refrain from frequent shifts in priority or delivery promises inconsistent with capability. Frequent changes in priorities result in frequent schedule changes, which is equivalent to no schedule. A management edict to load the schedule beyond actual capability results in more not-ready-to-ship items and fewer shipments unless priorities are firmly and clearly established and adhered to.

To meet the requirements for the bills of materials, engineers must be concerned about the manufacturing process beyond their normal engineering functions. They must maintain communication regarding changes to existing bills, new designs, and special manufacturing requests for additional part number designations or the restructuring of all existing bills. If this is not done or parts are missing from the bills, they are not ordered and the final product is delayed. If the control points are not properly established, the system will have to be supplemented with conventional expediting, the very thing that should be avoidable with a proper system.

Integrity of status data is undoubtedly the most difficult prerequisite for a successful MRP system, and it is usually given the least attention until after the system is implemented unsuccessfully. To achieve a sufficient level of accuracy every person handling the physical material or processing data must learn a new discipline. Secured physical facilities for storage must be provided. Precise procedures for documenting all material movements must be developed and compliance ensured. All personnel must be taught the procedures and supported with helpful audits of input data for several months until everyone is thoroughly proficient. Classroom training alone is not sufficient.

After this level has been achieved, a physical inventory must be taken to introduce new accurate balances into the debugged organization, manual procedures, and computer system with reasonable hope for maintaining accurate balances. If it is not already in operation, cycle counting of physical inventories and reconciliation to the records must be instituted to measure the accuracy achieved and to improve procedures as necessary to achieve the 95 percent level of accuracy. Implementation of MRP prior to this point guarantees chaos and results in late shipments, reduced productivity, more shortages and expediting, and higher inventory investment.

Many other elements are necessary for a successful and efficient MRP system but, unless grossly inaccurate, they do not prevent the system from functioning. Lead times, safety stocks, and order quantities, for instance, can vary significantly without precluding the success of the system.

A successful MMIS normally requires three to five years to develop and implement. Before embarking on a program, the entire management should require a complete simulation of the proposed system as it applies to that particular organization. A thorough detailed study of the simulation should be made to verify whether the system will operate satisfactorily on the computer within necessary turnaround times at expected volumes, what input data must be provided and how they must be provided, and whether output reports are adequate, with particular stress on management information. In addition, such a study should show what changes in organization, physical storage, and operating procedures will be required; what it will cost to start up and operate the system, including equipment, software, added personnel in data processing, materials control, production, engineering, purchasing, and all other departments, as well as additional materials handling and storage facilities if required; and whether hardware and software vendors and consultants are sufficiently committed to support all aspects.

When detailed systems development and implementation plans are fully determined and accepted, management must commit to the very essential long-term active direction and evaluation until each module is a proven success. Shifting to other more advanced systems at midstream can prolong completion dates indefinitely and should be avoided.   □ *Lamont M. LaRobardier*

FACILITIES PLANNING

By outlining a concrete method for facilities planning, it is hoped to make tangible what is inherently a rather nebulous task. Although the accent may appear to be on the method of planning, it should be understood that the quality and intensity of thinking used in preparing and executing the basic plan are more important than the precise procedure employed.

The Planning Team

Any program aimed at the planning and expeditious completion of a new facility or major improvements to an existing one should be thoroughly organized and should start with selection of the planning staff or team. This should be an integrated team that would include individuals having experience in such areas as plant layout, processing and packaging, equipment selection, materials handling, inventory control, and efficient warehousing. There will be an additional distinct advantage if the group includes those with experience and abilities in the development of new equipment and modifications to existing equipment, assuring that the new facility will be capable of operating at maximum profit and be sufficiently flexible to permit economical response to the dynamics of future product demands.

Ideally, all members of the planning group—but especially the leader—should possess additional attributes. The leader should be imaginative, with an analytical flair; he should have a proven affinity to the broad viewpoint (not merely expressed interest) and have the ability of objective judgment based on sound evaluations.

In this age of constant change, intense competition, and ever-increasing complexities, such primary attributes are the extra insurance against obtaining a facility that is just a duplicate of an existing operation rather than one capable of meeting today's technological challenges

Charting the Program

Although the tasks and activities to be performed will vary among companies and industries, the planning and programming remain a vital function of the planning team. The initial task should be the development and arrangement of a master guide that will cover the sequence of steps that must be undertaken in performance of the entire program.

The work tasks in each of the guide steps should be grouped together on a phased project basis. The advantages of well-defined steps and phases are that they provide preestablished checkpoints at which progress can be formally measured and present and future objectives reassessed in light of the latest findings, costs, and schedule projections; efficient utilization of technical personnel to assure maximum depth of project coverage at minimum cost; savings in time and money in nonproductive areas such as orientation, communication, administration, and coordination; optimum sequencing and scheduling of work in performing the planned tasks to avoid duplication of effort and unnecessary stoppage and delays.

The factors that should be covered in the overall plan and included in the master guide are as follows: (1) statements of the company's objectives in determining that a facility is to be established; (2) a program of developments or activities to be undertaken to attain these objectives; (3) a summary of the requirements generated by these developments; (4) a time schedule and assignments of responsibilities for accomplishing the various segments of the planning; (5) a plan for accomplishment, including a means of measuring progress; (6) calculations of cost (capital and expense) and return on investment; (7) a means of evaluating overall performance.

Stating the Objectives and Organizing the Tasks

The starting point of an effective plan for a new or improved facility is the development of comprehensive statements of management's objectives as to the kind and scope of manufacturing that will be undertaken; the required production capacity in terms of units of products to be produced per given period of time; the limitations, if any, to the size of the investment; and the time allotment within which the facility must be planned, procured, set up, and put into operation.

Once the objectives have been clearly documented and accepted by management, the second step in the master guide can be undertaken. This requires the determination and organization of a series of tasks and actions necessary to obtain the objectives. These too will vary by companies and industries as to details; however, the basic tasks will be similar.

A very helpful means of setting up the program of tasks is to develop a network diagram showing the sequence of activities and events required to achieve each of the planned objectives. Such a network provides not only an excellent means of programming but also of controlling the entire project. Two modestly sophisticated systems used extensively by many companies for planning major projects are PERT (program evaluation and review technique) and CPM (critical path method), both of which are discussed in Section 10 of this Handbook. There are other systems equally useful, although somewhat more sophisticated, which combine features of CPM and a Gantt chart. Substantial published information on all these systems is readily available to those who are not already familiar with them. The use of such methods as network diagramming of the tasks to be performed permits development of factors 2, 3, and 4 of the master guide in combination. If CPM is used, factor 6 can also be included. As an alternative to any of the standard systems, the planning group may devise a method for organizing its program of activities. Many planning groups prefer this approach.

The reasons prompting a need for the facility can be many and varied. There will, very likely, be a need to make some alterations in the planning program as the execution of tasks takes place; but these alterations will generally be few, compared to the essential tasks that must be part of any facilities planning program. These changes, additions, or deletions in total tasks will be almost automatic—or, at least, they will be obvious when the project motives are known.

Facility Location

The area location of the plant and the selection of a site should be early considerations as performance is initiated on the programmed tasks. If the primary reason for a new facility is, for example, expansion for increased capacity or the consolidation of several separate operations into a single efficient plant, a location that can best serve the whole market area or a specific segment of it must be the first concern. The plant must be economically accessible to the supply lines of raw materials and be centrally located within the area to be served in order to minimize distribution costs and time. The necessary facilities and means to effect the distribution must be readily available or easily obtainable. Local availability of services such as light, power, water, and the like must be investigated and evaluated.

Of major importance will be the local labor market and any of its conditions that might have a bearing on plant potential: the type, amount, and availability of labor; local union conditions, favorable or unfavorable, that could affect the operation; the possibility that this plant will be required to expand at a later date, and the adequacy of the site for expansion; the zoning restrictions and local or state tax laws that could be beneficial or detrimental to the operation; and the need for employee parking facilities—a "must" in this motorized age. These are but a few of the items that must be considered, investigated, documented, and evaluated. There will, however, be others, depending on the individual company's requirements and objectives.

Product Analysis

The kind of manufacturing that is to take place in the facility will have a significant bearing on the layout. It is therefore essential that the planning team have complete knowledge of all products to be produced in the plant and a thorough understanding of each operation to be performed on these products, both current and future. Look closely at all operations, with the aim of finding the ones that can be modified to simplify the work or the equipment required. Also look for instances where two or more operations can be done in combination to reduce manpower needs and machinery.

The starting point in this portion of the program should be with the products to be produced: their number and variety; variations within each type of product line, and their extensiveness; and any items so different that separate production equipment must be made available. For example, to obtain satisfactory marketing volume, a conveyor manufacturer must manufacture various types of equipment. Some types, such as gravity rollers and wheel conveyors, will utilize a minimum of manufacturing space, equipment, and worker skills. Items such as belt or slat conveyors, vertical conveyors, overhead chain systems, and other types of powered units require greater skills as well as more and different types of production equipment.

The volume in numbers of units produced would usually be greater in the gravity line than in the powered line. Both are needed, in the conveyor company's case, to meet market demands for combinations of both. Under such circumstances, greater efficiency can be achieved if the layout is designed to provide separate areas for each type of production. Such a requirement, however, will make it more difficult to plan the layout around straight line flow principles. Fortunately, with today's advances in handling techniques and the great variety of handling devices and means of application, the problems of staggered departments and operations within a system can be greatly minimized.

Plant Capacity Requirements

Before finalizing the product analysis, consider the projected volumes of each product. Determine whether there are any seasonal variations that could affect production or any styling problems that would require flexibility in the producing areas to permit such changes as can occur, for example, in a garment or sporting goods plant. Determine whether the finished products are made of separate components treated individually as subassemblies to be finally joined to other subassemblies into a finished item at final assembly. What is the makeup of materials that go into production? What are their forms? Are they solid, liquid, or bulk? Can the materials be easily handled both into and out of the various operations? What manual labor is necessary, or can automatic handling means be employed for the movement between operations? Detailed process flow charts should be prepared for each product line; they should include both the operations sequence and the average time period spent by the product or part at each stage.

There is a basic reason for beginning plant layout development with an analysis of the products to be manufactured. The findings of the analysis, when documented in orderly fashion, will outline the basic departments and areas that have to be provided for in the layout. It will remain for the planning group to determine the amount of plant space the separate departments will require and the relative position of each that will contribute most to a smooth flow of production through the facility. At the conclusion of this task, a clear picture will emerge as to the capacity assumptions on which the new facility is to be based.

All product information should be documented for each product—preferably, in detailed process chart form; from these records decisions can be made regarding both flow of work through the plant and production machinery requirements.

Production Flow

In the ideal flow arrangement, raw materials are received at one end of a plant, are fed directly to the first operation, and proceed in a straight line through successive operations until the finished product goes directly out of the plant to the customer. Such a manufacturing manager's dream will not be readily located, but an approach to it as a target will be helpful in the consideration of work flow.

Most manufacturing operations have a variety of raw materials that must be received in quantities and held in raw materials inventory storage. Similarly, finished products are rarely shipped directly from the final operation but usually go into finished-goods inventory storage from which shipments originate. One of the early considerations must be concerned with this procedure as work flow is analyzed.

Determine the size of the inventory of manufacturing materials that must be carried. Study its space requirements and the size of lots and their frequency of reception. Are the materials easily handled, and can standard materials-handling equipment be utilized to receive and place them in accessible storage, easily retrievable with a minimum of manual labor? How much truck dock or railroad siding space will be needed? Can warehousing be in the open, or must it be in an enclosure? Must it be heated or cooled? These and similar questions in connection with the finished-products warehousing requirements must be answered and the findings analyzed. Is the movement of goods, both in and out, sufficiently infrequent and staggered to permit utilization of common receiving and shipping facilities? Are the storage and handling such that the same personnel can perform both functions without undue congestion? For reasons of economy, if for no other, this is preferable; but it is not always attainable.

If the findings permit common facilities for the warehousing chores, considerable initial investment savings can be made in plant construction and utilization of available site area. If the findings indicate a marginal condition, an exhaustive investigation should be made of available handling and storing equipment, as well as scheduling flexibilities that might assist in overcoming the objectionable features of a common receiving and shipping department. Under no circumstances, however, should a compromise be made in the hope that future changes in movement patterns or equipment will permit the desired arrangement. While initial investments will be lower, any savings will quickly vanish if congestion in the warehousing departments causes production limitations and delays to finished-goods delivery.

If the original objectives assumed separate processing equipment for each of the product lines, review the reasons behind these objectives. Perhaps considerations of interchangeability of machinery (packaging equipment, for example) between product lines should be included as a consideration. Very often, substantial economies are made possible by planning joint use of equipment; thus evaluations of these interactions, after the basic requirements and process flow data have been obtained, can be desirable. While the planning and procurement time may be lengthened somewhat to accomplish the additional investigations, the results in many cases can be of major significance.

Facilities Layout

Once plant location has been determined, a site established, and the products to be produced thoroughly analyzed, the next activity on which to concentrate is plant layout. Resist the natural tendency to simplify the job by duplicating an existing facility, even if the facility has a good record for efficient operation. Strive for improvement; it is a rare case where improvements cannot be effected. Find the weak points and areas in an existing plant that need correction; then copy only the good ones when and if they fit into the plan.

If careful consideration is given to all pertinent matters applying to the facility, several alternative plant layouts will be formulated. These general layout concepts should initially be illustrated in block area layout drawings. The layouts will provide a basis for the general evaluation of the various concepts for analysis of flow process requirements, general operating economics, and potential capital cost.

In the course of developing layouts for the facility, consideration must be given to whether the planning will proceed along lines of a functional, process, or product-line layout. A product-line layout may require duplicate equipment for separate product lines, thus leading to increased capital investment. On the other hand, the functional type of layout will frequently introduce operational problems associated with the scheduling of different products through a common department. This can become a serious problem if one or more of the products are subject to rapid and extreme fluctuations in demand or have product characteristics that will restrict the allowable size of inventory. There is thus the possibility that a combination of functional and product-line layouts may be most appropriate, especially in the packaging areas.

In association with the planning functions for the type of layout concept being developed, the incorporation of proper materials handling must be considered. This subject was discussed previously in this section under "Materials Handling and Warehousing."

Automation

In the planning program, include allowances for investigation into the possibilities for automation of processing operations. Each year sees major advances in the techniques of making operations that traditionally have been manual completely automatic. In addition to the labor-saving potential possible through automation, there are many times when quality control, higher production volumes, and improvements in customer service resulting from automation within manufacturing can produce profit improvements of major magnitude. Consider also the improvement possibilities in semiautomation, especially in those functions that will not show economic justification for complete automation. In many instances, providing mechanical or electronic assists to an operator will maximize that operator's performance to such a degree that full automation could not be justified. Such items as automatic positioning and holding devices, parts feeders, and inspection devices in an assembly operation are assists that often permit one operator to control a production process formerly requiring two or more people.

Warehousing Requirements

There is a growing tendency for customers to insist on smaller shipments of merchandise delivered at more frequent intervals. This minimizes their need to provide warehousing facilities and reduces long-term investment in merchandise. It does, however, place a responsibility on the manufacturer to compensate with larger storage facilities and more complicated scheduling of outgoing products. Here again, the nature of the company's operation and the industry will have a major influence on decisions.

Planning Modifications

Frequent reference to the objectives developed in the first step of the master guide should be made in order to be certain that any decisions reached in the various stages of overall planning meet these objectives. This also serves another purpose. Very often, findings and conclusions in any of the planning areas will show sufficient advantages, either economically or functionally, to make changes in earlier decisions—and even, under some circumstances, in the objectives—worthwhile. For example, one company, faced with increasing demands by customers for smaller and more frequent shipments while the firm was still under the handicap of having to produce its products in large quantities because of the heavy cost of manufacturing changeovers, brought in the marketing department for consultation. A resulting alteration in marketing policy made it sufficiently advantageous to customers to order in large quantities and accept less frequent deliveries.

Final Plant Layout, Equipment, and Building Specifications

Allow provision in the program of tasks for the preparation of reports outlining the conclusions reached for each planning function. These reports will form the summary of recommended actions that can be taken and provide a basis for the final evaluation.

The most attractive of the alternative plant layouts should now be compared and evaluated in considerably greater detail. More precise cost estimates should be developed. Equipment and structural costs should be based upon price information from equipment manufacturers and construction firms. Explore also the ability of each of the alternative layout concepts to meet any probable future contingencies.

The actual selection of equipment for processing, warehousing, and packaging should be based upon a comprehensive study of economic and utility factors—cleanliness, safety, minimum machinery downtime, potential for product breakage if the products are fragile, ease of maintenance, and operational flexibility to meet possible future production requirements.

From the information developed in the summary reports, a detailed rating and evaluation of the most attractive plant and equipment layouts can then be prepared. Capital and operating costs, flexibility, ease of operation, cleanliness, and adaptability to expansion will be among the factors considered. On the basis of these findings, the final recommended layout can be developed. It may be one of the original alternatives or a combination of the better elements of several. The report should include a discussion of the reasons for the selection and, after it has been finalized, should be presented to management for review, comment, and approval.

With approval from management and appropriations for construction and procurement, the final facilities layout can be detailed to define the equipment to be procured and the building specifications to house the operation. If the project is of major size and includes a great number of operating segments, a further in-depth analysis of each segment should be made in an effort to maximize the possibilities for cost savings. Develop such information as the following: optimal concepts of equipment and method for each segment of the operation; an economic appraisal of each optimal concept in relation to present practices; detailed specifications of the selected concept in terms of equipment and operating requirements; an analysis of reaction time of source vendors or raw-materials suppliers (in some instances, on-hand inventories can be kept at absolute minimum if vendor reaction time is short and dependable); and a review of the company's attitudes toward production leveling and inventory size. Here the tradeoffs between a stable production force and inventory size will be tempered by considerations of such items as investment in products, product shelf life, and cost of storage facilities.

Procurement and Installation

In the summary report covering the final facilities layout, the equipment needed for operation should be listed with emphasis on items that need long lead times for delivery. Procurement efforts should be started with these items to minimize delays in final plant completion. In some instances, certain items may be ordered even before determination of the final layout.

This final phase of the program will include the procurement of all materials, equipment, and facilities and their installation in accordance with the preferred layout. Wherever possible, all elements of the plant should be tested and any required corrections made before turning them over to the operating department. Ideal conditions permit putting the entire plant into trial production operation before final acceptance. This procedure serves two purposes: It permits the training and evaluation of operating personnel and also provides a period of time to review the concepts in operating form and make changes or corrections that appear to offer improvements. A well-planned program will include in its time schedule such a period for run-in and testing.

Exact procedures for each step in the procurement and installation phase would be very difficult to set up. Much depends upon the industry, the nature and volume of products to be produced, the services to be provided, whether the items produced are finished products or just components, and many similar considerations. The general overall actions, however, are covered in the following areas of work effort: the purchase of capital equipment, including building; the design of modifications to standard equipment and processes, plus supervision of the modifications; the supervision of equipment installation and testing of operation in accordance with acceptance test specifications; the startup and debugging of the equipment and system; the completion of operating and maintenance manuals and spare parts lists; and continued liaison with plant operating management during the early periods of production.

Frequently, during this period, assistance can be given to plant operations on such topics as inventory control and optimum transportation arrangements and facilities for finished goods.

Upon the completion of the planned facility, when all equipment and processes are in operation and have been thoroughly debugged, a summary report should be prepared. It should include an outline of all actions taken and tasks performed, with an explanation of any major or unusual decisions. The report can provide a source of reference in the event of future changes to plant or products. It will also serve as a guide in planning any new or additional facilities and thus expedite the planning function by minimizing the initial work.

□ *Joseph F. O'Hora*

ENERGY MANAGEMENT

For many years, energy management programs took a back seat to other priorities in much of American industry. Fuel was abundant and cheap, and conservation programs had to compete for corporate funds with projects that offered better returns on investment—more plant capacity, increased research, additional office space, and new, computerized design, inventory, and manufacturing systems.

This situation was reversed dramatically during the 1970s with the oil embargo and the energy price shocks that followed during the decade. As the price of energy escalated, industrial managers came to realize that energy conservation could show very attractive returns, measured by any financial index. Tight corporate financial controls began working to the advantage of energy management, since well-managed conservation programs were making significant contributions to the bottom line.

For many U.S. companies, energy management and conservation has now become a way of life—with striking results. In 1979, the U.S. Office of Industrial Programs reported that "American industry has emerged as a leading practitioner of improved energy conservation and management." According to the report, targeted industries had improved their energy efficiency by an average of 15.4 percent over 1972. In 1979 alone, the reporting companies saved 2.2 quadrillion BTUs—the equivalent of over one million barrels of oil *per day*—compared to what they would have used at their 1972 levels of energy per unit of output.

This kind of conservation translates into substantial dollar savings. One diversified manufacturing company (3M), for example, reduced its energy consumption per unit of production by more than 29 percent between 1973 and 1980. The capital investment for 3M's energy conservation program during those years was $18.6 million, but the savings in energy costs amounted to $62 million. In 1980, 3M's conservation efforts saved the equivalent of 47 million gallons of fuel oil—enough to run the company for over a year.

In the ten years between 1970 and 1980, industrial energy management grew from a small and largely unrecognized movement to become a major profit center for American industry.

The Energy Manager

A successful energy management program involves much more than simply turning off lights and adding insulation. Ideally, it should be a total program that involves every area of the business—research, process development, manufacturing, marketing, and financial and strategic planning. It must also reach outside the company, to include suppliers, customers, various government and legislative agencies, and the general public.

A program as complicated as this demands an unusual mix of skills from its managers, ranging from purely technical expertise to a flair for marketing and salesmanship. Here are some of the areas a good energy manager must master:

Technical expertise. Energy management always begins with a solid technical background, preferably in mechanical, electrical, or plant engineering. Managers need a good grasp of both theory and the nuts-and-bolts details of conservation programs. This includes a thorough understanding of the company's processes, products, maintenance procedures, and facilities.

Communication. In the course of a single week, energy managers might find themselves dealing with lawyers, engineers, accountants, financial planners, public relations specialists, government officials, and even journalists and legislators. A good energy manager has to be able to communicate clearly and persuasively with all of these people—in their own language. Above all, energy managers must be able to sell the benefits of their programs to top management. Without firm and continuing support from the top, their programs are destined for failure in the competition for corporate funds and attention.

Financial understanding. To enlist the support of top management, energy managers have to develop and present their programs as investments, with predictable returns, instead of as unrecoverable costs. They have to demonstrate what kind of returns—in both energy and cost savings—can be expected from each project, and over what period of time. This means, first of all, developing some credible way to measure returns—a method that can be understood and accepted by the financial officers of the company.

Planning and strategy. A basic part of energy management is forecasting future energy supplies and costs with reasonable accuracy. This means coming to grips with the complexities of worldwide supply, market trends, demand projections, and the international political climate. There is no way, of course, to predict all of these things with certainty, but every business, especially energy-intensive ones, will need some kind of reliable forecasting from now on.

Community relations. Energy managers have some responsibility to go outside their companies to share their ideas and experience with a variety of publics. Trade and professional associations can become clearinghouses for new ideas. Legislatures and government agencies need, and often welcome, expert help in setting standards and policies. And the public needs help in understanding what is at stake in learning to use our limited supplies of energy wisely and efficiently.

Energy managers should formulate and implement programs to ensure a steady supply of energy and to reduce costs wherever possible. Those programs have five main components: a plan to ensure a reliable energy supply for all operations, complete energy audits of each facility, a complete energy conservation program for each facility, engineering standards for new construction and for retrofitting existing buildings, and an accurate reporting system to measure results.

Energy Supply

Obviously, the first priority of any energy program is to ensure a steady and adequate supply of energy for the company's facilities. This is not always easy, since shortages in both power and fossil fuels have become facts of life in America. Energy managers cannot control these outside forces, but they can plan to minimize their impact.

Power Shortages

The demand for electrical power in the United States continues to grow, even though the rate of growth has declined in the past few years. Unfortunately, the capacity to generate power is not keeping pace with the growth in demand. As a result, many electrical-power users have experienced shortages, brownouts, and blackouts, and there is every indication that these interruptions will continue in the foreseeable future. That cannot be helped. What is important is to meet these shortages with a plan, instead of with panic.

A power curtailment plan should have two basic parts: (1) a liaison procedure between the site and the power company, and (2) a plan to deal with actual curtailments.

One person at every facility should be formally designated as liaison person with the local power company. This would normally be the maintenance manager, but it could be anyone thoroughly familiar with the site's needs. If the power company does not contact its customers about long-range plans for power curtailment, the liaison person should take the initiative to establish communication with the utility. It is critical for the power company to know exactly whom to deal with in an emergency.

In most cases, the power company will have at least two brownout procedures. The first will be a request to reduce power to a level that will be enough to keep plant production in operation but that may cause some inconvenience and discomfort. The second would suspend production and feed the site only enough power to support security and maintenance.

Often, if a plant fails to comply with the first brownout request, the power company will impose the second, more drastic procedure. In any case, the site needs plans to cope with both situations, including the necessary delegation of authority and responsibility.

The liaison person should have primary responsibility for developing procedures and specific assignments to deal with a brownout, including a plan for rapid communication with all managers and supervisors in an emergency. If conditions become critical, he should remain in close touch with the power company throughout the emergency.

When a request to reduce power is received, the liaison should immediately begin activating the site plan. He should first authenticate the request through his contact at the power company. The next step is to check with the site manager for approval, and then put the plan into action by contacting the responsible people throughout the site. The liaison is also responsible for starting normal operations again, once the power company tells him the emergency has passed.

This whole procedure rests on thorough preplanning. Before an emergency is declared, someone—probably the maintenance department—must inventory all the kinds of power in use at the company facilities, and decide which ones are most vulnerable to interruption, and what would happen if power is restricted, either gradually or abruptly.

Decide in advance which equipment can be turned off or restricted if power is reduced gradually. During a brownout, for example, some air conditioners and air-handling units can be turned off or turned down; lighting can be reduced in storage areas, mechanical equipment rooms, and other unoccupied areas; elevators can be stopped; and the temperature of chilled-water systems can be raised if there is no load-limit control. During a fuel shortage, thermostats can be lowered in stairwells, corridors, and some production areas; heat can be turned off in unoccupied areas; and nonproduction equipment can be shut down.

Fossil-fuel Shortages

Shortages in fossil fuels, caused by events far beyond any manager's control, may also be a fact of life for years to come. When they happen, commercial and industrial establishments often feel the pinch first. Many legislatures have established allocation systems that protect private homes from shortages as long as possible and cut off manufacturing plants first.

The first objective for any site during a fuel shortage is to continue production at acceptable standards for as long as possible. The time to make these plans is long before a shortage occurs.

The first step here is to analyze the use of fossil fuels throughout the plant to determine the impact of a shortage on each operation during both short- and long-term disruptions, the effect on related operations (such as possible quality problems), the effect on overall production, and the time needed to recover and restore the production rate.

The next step is to develop contingency plans that outline workable procedures to minimize the effects of an interruption on production levels and on the space environment Here are some typical procedures to reduce comfort and process loads:

Comfort Space Conditions

Lower thermostats in spaces to the lowest temperature which is tolerable for the function being performed.

Lower thermostat settings in unoccupied spaces.

Lower temperature in stairwells and corridors.

Shut down air-handling units serving areas of limited use.

Shut off supply of heat to rooms which may be heated by solar radiation through windows or which may receive heat from adjacent areas.

Lower the air or hot water supply temperature for heating to the lowest point necessary to provide minimum required heating.

Reduce exhaust air quantities to a minimum.

Reduce outside air to provide makeup for exhaust air requirements only.

Turn off humidifiers where possible.

Reduce or eliminate any introduction of moisture for humidification in corridors, storerooms, equipment rooms, lounges, lobbies, kitchens, etc.

Shut off energy source for domestic hot water heating system. (Note: Codes may require a minimum temperature for dishwashing.)

Shut off domestic hot water circulating pump.

Regulate outdoor air dampers to utilize outdoor air for cooling the building when the temperature is adequate.

Shut down unneeded equipment such as water coolers, dispensing equipment, and business machines.

Process

Cut back, where possible, any loads on the interrupted fuel which would help to reduce consumption.

Transfer loads from the uninterrupted fuel to an energy supply which is more readily available.

Substitute an alternative fuel for the interrupted fuel.

Delay or reduce energy-intensive steps in processes until the supply of the critical fuel can be restored to a normal level.

Consider drawing from inventory as a means for reducing process requirements which are energy-intensive.

Shut down gas-consuming equipment not required for production.

Stagger use of equipment such as furnaces, heat treating, process heating, etc.

Shift portions of production to hours when energy supply can be renewed.

Every facility should appoint a site energy representative who will be responsible for working out an implementation program and putting it into action during an emergency. Specifically, the site energy representative should (1) work with suppliers to estimate as well as possible their ability to meet the site's energy requirements and investigate each supplier's history of curtailment, the length and frequency of the outages, and the advance notice given to customers; (2) verify the supplier's emergency allocation plan and make sure that the supplier is able to restore service promptly after an emergency interruption; (3) determine the limits on the supply of certain fuels and compare them with the future needs of the plant, paying special attention to the production rates and reserves of natural gas suppliers; (4) make sure that distribution networks have multiple sources and loopfeed capability; and (5) review government plans for fuel emergencies, especially for fuels that are critical to the plant.

One of the most important, and most difficult, jobs of the site energy representative is to look ahead and try to anticipate future fuel shortages. These shortages can come from many directions. Suppliers of gas, fuel oil, coal, or electricity may be unable to make scheduled deliveries. Legislatures or Congress could declare an emergency and limit the use of certain fuels, or rule out any use during certain times of the day.

There is no way to anticipate everything that could happen. But meticulous planning and careful forecasting can go a long way toward helping any company make the best of a bad situation.

Energy Audits

An energy audit is a complete report on energy use and cost and on opportunities for conservation at a particular plant, office building, warehouse, or other facility. Auditors need the following information to start: (1) an energy history, listing gas, coal, oil, and electrical use for the past several years, (2) an energy cost projection for the next five years, to be used to estimate potential savings, (3) a complete set of mechanical, electrical, and process drawings, including prints of plant layouts and plan views of major equipment rooms, and (4) lists of all major equipment, showing energy demands, motor horsepower, design conditions, and air flows.

The auditors analyze all energy-using systems in the plant or building—mechanical, electrical, process, and general construction. They prepare flow diagrams that document where the energy is used, and check all major process systems, HVAC (heating, ventilating, and air-conditioning) systems, lighting levels, and major components to verify actual operating conditions. When they have collected and analyzed all this information, the auditors recommend energy conservation opportunities (ECOs)—specific retrofit projects, repairs and maintenance, and changes in operations that will save energy. Every ECO should have an estimate of projected costs and savings based on simple payback calculations.

Finally, the auditors classify the ECOs into *recommended* projects (those which will meet your individual investments criteria) and *deferred* projects (those which do not meet your payback requirements).

Energy audits are an indispensable management tool for any energy conservation program. Without them, the projects will be haphazard and based on guesswork. With an accurate audit, managers can tell exactly what needs to be done, how much it will cost, and what they can expect for their money. Site-specific energy cost projections for five years in the future are recommended for inclusion in the calculation of project ROIs.

Individual Energy Conservation Programs

Every facility needs its own conservation program. No single set of recommendations can cover every manufacturing plant, laboratory building, office complex, warehouse, and sales and distribution center. Once the energy audit is completed, corporate energy managers should work with local management to tailor an individual program for the specific location.

Corporate management can provide general guidelines and suggestions, but local managers have to decide whether the recommendations are compatible with their standards for safety, engineering, insurance, process, and the comfort of employees.

The following recommendations can provide a general framework for designing individual energy conservation programs. The recommendations for each category are divided into three sections: (1) operation and adjustment—those items which can be done immediately without special personnel; (2) maintenance —those items which can be done by plant maintenance people without outside help; and (3) system modifications—those items which require engineering involvement, and would probably have to be installed with the help of an outside contractor.

General

Operation and Adjustment

Reduce compressed air pressure to the minimum required. Higher pressures require more horsepower to compress, more leakage is apt to occur, and usage will be greater since high pressure is more difficult to accurately control manually.

Operate air-handling systems only when needed. The starting times should be varied with the load for heating and cooling systems. During peak heating or cooling times, the system should be started earlier than during intermediate weather.

Run only the equipment needed; for example, do not run two boilers or chillers, etc.

Discourage unnecessary passenger elevator use.

Discourage the use of compressed air for personnel cooling. Provide fans.

Maintenance

Disconnect unused steam or compressed air branches. The compressed air branches in all probability leak and the steam mains lose heat to the space.

Conserve water by installing inexpensive flow controllers. These flexible orifice-type controllers are available in ½ gpm increments, up to 5 gpm.

Check and calibrate heating, cooling, and ventilation controls at least seasonally.

Repair building cracks with caulking or other suitable means. Weatherstrip doors. In general, seal the building.

Repair leaking faucets or, better yet, replace them with spring-closing water-saver-type faucets.

Install time clocks to start and stop equipment to avoid operation when not required.

Install a plastic sheet over poorly fitted windows or skylights.

Close off unused floor space or rooms to save heating, cooling, and ventilation.
Close unused openings with insulated panels.
Consider use of electric-driven motors in place of compressed air motors.
Provide water treatment for hydronic heating and cooling systems to improve heat transfer.

Systems Modifications

Try to find a use for once-through cooling water that has been warmed, such as, for washing or as makeup for boilers or cooling tower.
When replacing single-pane windows or reroofing, consider installing double-pane windows and adding roof insulation.
Increase maker speed to increase efficiency.

Heating

Operating and Adjustment

Maintain room temperature no higher than 70° F in offices, 65° F in operating departments, and 50° F in warehouses, and maintain humidity no higher than 20 percent rh unless a process requires some other temperature or humidity. During unoccupied periods, the temperature should be set 10° F lower in offices and operating departments.
Set domestic water heater temperature at 110° F.

Maintenance

Repair leaking steam traps. A trap can be checked by an infrared heat detector to see if the inlet and outlet are the same temperature; no movement on the heat detector indicates that the trap leaks.
Install shrouds on dock doors to minimize cold air infiltration.
Consider using fuel oil additives to improve combustion.
Install time clocks to start and stop equipment to avoid unnecessary operation.
Repair damaged insulation, weatherstripping, or caulking.

System Modifications

Recirculate dust collector exhaust air by using filters to conserve heated air.
Steam being discharged to the atmosphere in any case is a waste. Consider heat recovery devices, find uses for low-pressure steam, repair leaking relief valves, etc.
When replacing burners or adding new ones, install dual-fuel capability to provide for future flexibility, where dual fuels are available.
Do not allow condensate to be wasted. Where hazardous materials are involved, use a heat exchanger rather than wasting the condensate.
Consider heat recovery from contaminated exhaust air or contaminated hot waste water with appropriate exchangers.
Use air compressor, inert gas generator, etc., spent cooling water as makeup for boilers or cooling tower.
Consider viscosity control on fuel oil heaters to allow flexibility in mixing fuel oils.

Keep boilers clean. Install soot blowers on oil-fired boilers. Use exhaust air for oven heater makeup. (Do not use exhaust air from hazardous areas.)

Consider installing lower-explosion-limit controlled oven air recirculation.

Provide an insulated shroud around kilns and provide partial recirculation of the hot air.

Install turbulators in boiler fire tubes to increase heat transfer efficiency.

Install glycol runaround or other heat exchanger to recover oven exhaust heat to heat the oven makeup air.

Investigate heat recovery from thermal oxidizers for heating oven makeup of supply air, or for generating steam.

Use heat from air-cooled air compressors, condensing units, etc., to provide space heating in the winter.

Install a closed system for cooling water for brakes on machinery to reduce water consumption and to provide an opportunity for heat recovery.

Utilize flash steam from a high-pressure process as low-pressure steam supplement for heating buildings.

Insulate heavy fuel oil storage tanks.

Cooling

Operation and Adjustment

Maintain room temperature no lower than 78° F and humidity no lower than 52 percent rh unless a process requires some other temperature or humidity. Room thermostats on reheat systems should be left at 70° F, the winter setting.

Raise chilled water temperature.

On DX (direct expansion) system, raise the suction temperature.

Adjust water control valves on city- or well-water cooled refrigerant condensers to maintain leaving water temperature no lower than 75° F to 85° F, to conserve water.

Set cooling tower fan control down to supply lowest practical water temperature (approximately 65° F) to reduce compressor power consumption.

Maintenance

Verify chilled water flow in cooling coils. The chilled water must be counter flow, that is, the chilled water must enter the coil on the leaving air side for maximum efficiency. The greater temperature difference with counter flow will lower the leaving air temperature up to 6° F.

Keep condensers clean. Blow lint out of air-cooled condenser coils to promote heat transfer, which will lower the head pressure, which will reduce the horsepower required by the compressor.

Adjust the temperature rise on cooling water to maximum allowable to conserve water.

Install awnings or sun-control films on windows to reduce solar heat gain.

Install an automatic brush-cleaning system on larger chiller condensers where condensers have to be cleaned frequently because of poor water.

System Modifications

Consider installing low-level cooling to avoid cooling the dead space near the ceiling, or installing spot cooling at work stations rather than totally cooling the complete area.

Consider using closed-loop chiller system for cooling in lieu of city water or well water.

Install controls on air-handling equipment so that mixed air dampers will introduce 100 percent outdoor air whenever the outdoor temperature is below the return air temperature. On large systems, use an enthalpy controller to sense total heat, including latent heat. On smaller systems, a dry bulb switchover point can be picked with an average wet bulb.

On reheat air-conditioning systems, install a control system that will "reset"; that is, vary the chilled water cooling discharge temperature and mixed air temperature according to temperature needed to maintain the space temperature setting.

Ventilation

Operation and Adjustment

Reduce exhaust air quantity to that which is actually needed to remove dust or odors. (However, general exhausts in hazardous areas must remain at the specified amount). Reduce fan speeds and shut off fans when not needed.

Maintenance

Repair air-handling unit housings and ductwork leaks by caulking or taping. Heated or cooled air which leaks into spaces not requiring heating or cooling is total waste of energy.

Verify correct rotation of fans. A fan running backward will discharge some air, but it is very inefficient.

Keep air filters clean. Dirty air filters waste energy by reducing air flow and reducing system efficiency.

Adjust the outdoor air intake damper so only the minimum amount of outdoor air is introduced during maximum heating and cooling periods. Do not reduce the outdoor air quantity below 5 cfm per occupant.

Reduce all heating, cooling, and exhaust fan speeds to the minimum required to satisfy peak space heating and cooling loads. The reduction in air quantity, cfm, is proportional to the fan speed and pulley diameter; therefore, the motor pulley size can be reduced incrementally to reduce the cfm until it matches the load.

System Modifications

Install exhaust hoods over heat-producing devices such as electric motors or MG sets to reduce the room cooling load. Install a bypass on the exhaust duct so that the heat can be discharged to the space when needed for heating.

Install heat recovery from hot exhaust air.

Consider using activated carbon filters to remove nontoxic odors from the air to reduce the amount of outdoor air required and make it possible to recirculate more return air.

Install an "unoccupied" cycle on air-handling equipment which will close the outside air damper during unoccupied hours. Or cycle the unit with a room thermostat, with the outdoor air damper closed to save fan power and outdoor air heating or cooling.

Install back draft dampers on exhaust fan discharges. CAUTION: Do not install on discharges which have stringy residues or contaminants—these could deposit upon the damper and make it inoperative.

Install a room static pressure controller to vary the amount of outdoor makeup air introduced into the space to match intermittent or varying exhaust load.

Lighting and Electrical

Operation and Adjustment

Instruct personnel to have lights on only when and where needed.

Schedule discretionary loads to off-peak hours to reduce peak demands.

Resistance heating units should not be kept hot continuously. They should be turned on only when needed, although the warm cycle should not be scheduled for the peak demand period.

Deenergize transformers whenever they are not in use.

Maintenance

Remove or disconnect light fixtures, or replace them with smaller or more efficient light fixtures to maintain proper lighting levels.

Provide adequate switching to permit reduction of lighting level when it is not needed.

When replacing an electric motor, install as small a motor as possible to match the load, to improve power factor and efficiency.

Also, consider installing two-speed motors where the load is variable, as in an air-conditioning unit fan which requires full capacity only a few days a year.

Clean lighting fixtures and relamp on a scheduled basis.

System Modifications

Consider installing capacitors to improve the system power factor.

Consider installing fluorescent or high-pressure sodium-vapor-type lights in place of incandescent.

Install photocells to control outdoor lighting.

Install high-level local lighting for high-intensity work areas to avoid overlighting the remainder of the area.

Monitor power demand for consideration of a peak shedding control system.

Engineering Standards

The ideal time to begin a conservation program is before a building is constructed or a process started. Energy managers can help build efficiency and cost savings into a project from the start, if they have a set of architectural, structural, and civil engineering conservation standards to work from. The same standards can be used as a guide to retrofitting existing buildings. Energy managers should seek professional guidance and advice from organizations such as the American

Society of Heating, Refrigerating, and Air-Conditioning Engineers (ASHRAE), 345 East 47th Street, New York, NY 10017.

Here are some specific suggestions for improving the energy efficiency of both new and existing buildings.

Site Development

Minimize length of on-site truck and auto runs.

Take advantage of terrain and surrounding environment to minimize impact on structure by wind and sun.

Landscape to provide wind protection and solar shading.

Analyze impact of building and room orientation on solar and wind control.

Locate high-energy consumption buildings near energy sources and disposal systems.

Mass buildings with common walls.

Use megastructures, not campus-style individual buildings.

Mass buildings for shade on adjacent windows.

Zigzag east and west arcades (glazing on south). Minimize winter wind effects, facilitate shading in summer and utilization of sun in winter.

Face sloping roofs to the south.

Use deciduous trees for solar control and reduced winter winds.

One or two floors below grade, use berming for protection.

Planning

Windowless north walls with minimal use space along north wall act as a buffer to north.

Take advantage of natural daylight.

Locate windows high in wall.

Provide exterior shades to eliminate direct sunlight.

Consider more extensive use of open office planning where practical to simplify environmental control systems. Studies indicate office landscaping consumed 25 percent less energy in lighting than partitioned offices.

Minimize windows, especially north elevations.

Locate windows on south facade for winter sun.

Locate rooms with highest process heat gain on walls with the highest exposure loss.

Group rooms to reuse air through other spaces.

Increase density of populations.

Group rooms needing special temperature and humidity requirements.

Make good use of reflective surfaces to enhance natural lighting.

Locate insulation on exterior of building if possible.

Use light colors on roof and exterior to reduce heat gain in summer.

Use roof sprays or roof ponds to reduce solar heat gain in summer, especially where process has high heat gain.

Design operable sash so that it does not exceed 25 percent of the glazed opening.

Use external solar control devices, as they are most effective.

Reduce heat gains through windows.

Shade from direct sun April through October.

Use wind protection for any exposed surface with a U greater than 0.20.

Protect insulation from moisture. Use insulation with low moisture absorption which regains thermal performance after being wet.

Use light wells and atriums. They let in daylight for illumination and for minimal heating and cooling loads, and they also lower wind effects and solar heat gain.

Avoid thermal bridge frames.

Use operable shutters to reduce U to 0.1 at glazing.

Avoid thermal bridges through exterior walls.

Insulate slab on grade. Use wall insulation to full depth of foundation wall, and equivalent insulation under first 4 feet of slab perimeter.

Reduce air infiltration. Use impermeable exterior surface materials.

Weatherstrip all exterior doors.

Locate building entrances on downwind side. Provide windbreak.

All entrances should have vestibules or revolving doors. Vestibules should have self-closing doors. Locate ventilation louvers on downwind side of building —use windbreaks.

Minimize environmental systems in all nonfunctional areas, e.g., storerooms, exit stairs, etc.

Minimize areas not used full-time, such as corridors and lobbies.

Analyze required ceiling heights to reduce impact on environmental systems.

Design

Analyze structural design to minimize use of basic raw materials.

Analyze wall systems and provide minimum U factor for the opaque wall surface for various heating-degree-day areas.

Provide double-glazed windows as a minimum for all buildings in the 3,000 to 9,000 heating-degree-day areas and on all air conditioned buildings in the 0–3,000 heating-degree-day range. Window areas should not exceed 15 percent of gross wall area.

Analyze roof systems and provide a minimum heat transmission.

Insulate exterior doors and access panels.

Analyze glazing and glazing retention systems to provide minimum solar gain and heat loss. Consider use of solar control devices.

Weatherstrip and windstop all openings and frame systems.

Perimeter foundation walls for slab-on-grade floors or heated space below grade should have a U transmission equal to standards set by ASHRAE.

Energy Conservation Analysis Procedure

Prepare an energy and cost-benefit analysis for all environmental systems and building components and materials as part of a schematic design using all architectural and engineering disciplines. The schematic phase is critical to eventual energy consumption. Also prepare an operating cost analysis on an annual basis as part of preliminary building estimates, and develop job procedures which will incorporate the system for analysis of new building projects.

Electrical Engineering

Lighting

□ Design the lighting systems for the expected activity. Install the light where it is needed for the seeing tasks, and reduce the levels in surrounding non-working area. Recommended lighting levels for various occupancies and uses are shown in Table 4-1.

Table 4-1. Lighting levels for task areas.

Area	Lighting Levels (fc)
Accounting	70
Design, drafting	70
Regular office work	70
Private offices	50
Corridors (minimum)	20
Lobby	30
Cafeterias	
Quick service	30
Kitchen	70
Leisure type	20
Toilet areas	30
Locker rooms	20
Libraries	70
Laboratories	70
Parking areas	0.3
Roadways	0.2
Warehouses	10–20
Converting	
Cutting and slitting	70
Service areas	40
Makers	
Winder, unwind	70
Inspection	70
Oven area	20
Maintenance area	
Fine work	70
Rough work	50
Mixing, milling, chemical reactors	50

SOURCE: 3M Company.

- Provide two-level lighting and switching to permit reduction in light intensities when the area is not in use. The potential energy savings may be substantial.
- Utilize daylight whenever possible and practical.
- Consider the efficiencies of the reflectors and lenses of the luminaires. A two-lamp 2-ft by 4-ft fixture has a coefficient of utilization (CU) of 0.79, whereas a four-lamp fixture has a CU of 0.71.
- Design switch circuits to permit turning off unused and unnecessary light. Cleaning operations do not require the same amount of lighting as office work, and controls should be provided for each local area. Circuits should be arranged with fixtures or lamps on alternate circuits with consideration for the maintenance lighting and general lighting.
- Arrange corridor lighting on two circuits for two levels of illumination with automatic timer to reduce light except when traffic is heavy. A two-circuit arrangement also applies to conference rooms, cafeterias, and multipurpose rooms such as labs, offices, and large mechanical spaces.
- Provide timers to turn off lights automatically in remote or little used areas, and provide manual time switches for stairways, closets, etc. Automatic shutdown could also apply to service corridors, mechanical spaces, and internal lighting for air supply units.
- Parking lots are often lighted all night for a few employees. Controlling the lighting in coordination with a security guard can eliminate leaving lighting on all night for a few people. Photocells and electric timers geared to working shifts of employees also may be effective.
- Arrange electrical systems to accommodate relocatable luminaires which can be removed to suit changing furniture layouts. This may require surface or pendant-mounted fixtures.
- Consider the use of fixtures wired so that lamps are connected end to end (tandem) to a ballast instead of side by side so that half-level illumination will not be spotty. A local switch or plug-in connection would permit "off" operation on selected fixtures. Use more efficient light sources. The variations in intensities measured in lumens per watt for different lamp types are shown in Table 4-2; Figure 4-24 compares efficiency of five types.
- Room return air passing across tubes removes 50 percent of the electrical heat of the fixture and reduces air-conditioning load of the space. Thermal-controlled luminaires increase light output by 10 percent.

Reduce Peak Electrical Demand

- Consider the use of more smaller-size motors to reduce the peak electrical demand. Properly size electric motors. Select horsepower for 110 percent of maximum full-load requirements. The more generously you size your prime mover, the more nonworking power you introduce into the system.
- Design and select machinery to start in an unloaded condition to reduce starting torque requirements. (For example, start pumps against closed valves.)

Table 4-2. Output for different lamp types.

Lamp Type	Output (Lumens/Watt)
Incandescent	16–20
Fluorescent	56–68
Mercury	22–51
Metal additive	65–98
High-pressure sodium	66–132
Low-pressure sodium	77–150

SOURCE: 3M Company.

□ Use direct drive whenever possible to eliminate drive train losses. Select motors that are not oversized for the load rating, so peak efficiency is realized.
□ Provide control to shut off recirculation pumps automatically during weekends, night, and periods of the day which are well defined, when hot water usage is light.
□ Utilize waste heat from transformers for beneficial use in other systems.

Figure 4-24. Comparison of savings (equivalent gallons of fuel oil per year) for five lighting sources in a typical new laboratory building. (Source: 3M Company.)

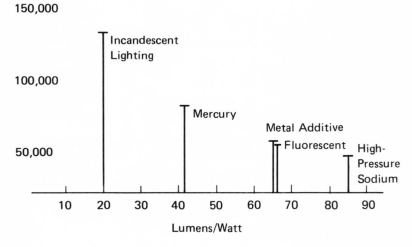

Large transformer units of the dry type may be located in mechanical spaces and ventilated mechanically through suitable heat extraction equipment.
□ Install capacitors to increase the system power factor.

Mechanical Engineering

□ Use minimum outdoor air. Design systems and controls to a minimum of 5–8 cfm per person outdoor makeup air unless local codes, process exhausts, and laboratory hood exhausts require more. When exhaust volumes vary considerably during daily operation, use static pressure-controlled outdoor air inlet dampers to assure minimum air makeup. Investigate the potential energy savings from reducing outdoor air makeup.

□ Where building ventilating, heating, cooling, and process requirements allow, use variable air volume systems.

□ Design all heating, ventilating, and air-conditioning (HVAC) units to use up to 100 percent outdoor air for cooling, whenever the space requires cooling and the outdoor air enthalpy is below the room enthalpy control point.

□ Use low- or medium-pressure air systems. Design air systems for static pressures of less than 6″ H_2O. High-pressure air systems require high fan horsepower.

□ Reuse heating from lights and solar gain. Transfer solar heat from south, east, and west sides of building to north, west, and east sides at appropriate times by use of a common return air plenum. Also use common plenum to utilize heat from lights plus interior loads supplied to the perimeter area.

□ Indoor design conditions for human comfort occupancy should be 78° F and 52 percent relative humidity for cooling and 70° F for heating. Process area design conditions should be the minimum required to maintain product quality.

□ Specify quality control components that are well characterized over the full turndown of the system. Provide a time clock, preferably seven-day, which will shut down the HVAC unit during periods when the building or area is unoccupied.

□ Provide exhaust fan and/or HVAC unit interlocks with process equipment to shut down equipment when the process is not in operation, except where ventilation system must operate for safety reasons.

□ Provide a master room thermostat for each HVAC unit, arranged to control directly and in sequence the mixed air dampers through the enthalpy controller, the preheat coils, the cooling coils, and the reheat coils to maintain the room temperature.

□ Consider central supervisory monitoring and control of HVAC units and process equipment to maximize operating and maintenance efficiencies for large building complexes.

□ Use shrouds on dock doors wherever possible. Consider air curtain fans when shrouds are not installed. Do not use dock heaters when warehouse is heated and pressured by air supply unit.

□ Select motor horsepower for no more than 110 percent of maximum brake horsepower requirements. Oversize motors result in poor efficiency and contribute to low system power factor.

□ Use the flash steam from high-pressure process coils for primary or preheat coils on the same process systems. If not feasible, then connect to a flash tank to feed the low-pressure steam system.

□ Design systems to recover all condensate. Where solvents or hazardous fluids are steam-heated, use a safety tube heat exchanger to eliminate possibility of condensate contamination. On condensate pump systems from flash tanks, use high-temperature transfer pumps and blend hot condensate (above 200° F) with cold condensate (140–180° F) in a condensate tank to eliminate or reduce the loss of vented flash steam.

□ Design hot water systems for domestic use at 110° F.

□ Utilize waste low-pressure steam. Evaluate economics of using waste steam for steam absorption units or for low-pressure turbines for refrigeration systems.

□ Evaluate the economics of using the refrigeration system for both cooling and heating. Consider the utility electrical rates and the source of energy used for generation as well as the winter process cooling loads. In some cases a good heat balance can be attained between heat given off by a refrigerant condenser and the plant heating demand.

□ Consider heat recovery or reuse from air exhaust. Incinerators, thermaloxidizers, process systems, toilet areas, electrical transformer rooms, kitchens, offices, laboratory hoods, equipment rooms, and computer rooms are all tangible sources of recovery. Reuse the exhaust air by transferring to other areas if the air is clean. Consider for reuse for stairways, penthouses, exterior corridors, loading docks, and warehouses. If you cannot reuse, then design for heat recovery using a rotary wheel air-to-air heat exchanger, closed-circuit system, fixed air-to-air heat exchanger, or heat pipe exchanger.

□ Consider heat recovery or reuse from liquids and waste products. Consider both sensible heat and possible generation of methane gas from sanitary sewers.

□ Consider using heat from clean-water sewers for either air or liquid transfer, or for the false load on mechanical refrigeration reverse cycle heat pump application.

□ Reuse clean water for other processor or for building mechanical equipment. Examples: Boiler makeup, lawn sprinkling, plant hot water, refrigerant condensers, quench for incinerators, heat pumps, and cooling tower makeup. If dry scrap solvents cannot be reclaimed, then consider feasibility of incineration utilizing a waste heat boiler. The steam generated would reduce the fuel consumption at the boiler house. If the clean solvents are of fairly constant calorific value, they could also be used as an alternative fuel for stationary boilers.

Water Conservation

The efficient use of water saves energy. One area with a high potential for energy savings is the use of air compressor after-cooler water for boiler makeup. Since this water is discharged at 95° F to 105° F, the savings in fuel required to bring regular water supplies from an average of 55° F to 95° F can be measured in thousands of gallons of fuel oil saved. In addition, sewerage charges for condenser water are eliminated, since boiler evaporation is non-chargeable.

Where a relatively low rate of rise on cooling is permitted, use a closed-circuit glycol or chilled water system to minimize or eliminate water usage. This is applicable in particular to oven rolls and bearings, cooling drums, mills, etc. These systems utilize large volumes of circulated media for the cooling necessary with a 3° F or 4° F rise. When this is translated into actual cooling load, a small chiller with a low electrical input can replace several hundred gallons per minute of cooling water.

Where process requires chilled water or domestic water for cooling, provide solenoids interlocked with process equipment. Provide flow control by thermostatic control of a valve.

Well water at 52° F can be used for cooling air to 64° F on the first pass, with water leaving temperature of 60° F. After leaving the coils, the water can be used for less critical areas to cool air to 74° F to maintain conditions of 80–82° F and 60 percent rh in work areas normally subjected to high ambient temperatures. The water could also be used for refrigerant condensing on chilled water or glycol systems. This condensing water at 80° F can be used for high-temperature process cooling, domestic nonpotable water, makeup water for cooling towers, or process mixing water for paper making, glue mixing, etc., where temperatures at 85° F or higher preclude the need for heating the makeup.

Boiler Systems

□ Recover heat from stack gasses. Use an economizer for preheating boiler feedwater or an air-to-air exchanger for preheating the combustion air.
□ Use steam, air, or water for obtaining maximum atomization and mixing of fuel and air.
□ Use automatic viscosity controllers on fuel oil systems to attain the best atomization for efficient combustion. This control also permits the flexibility of mixing and using any grade fuel oil, either distillate or residual.
□ Use proven additives to improve the efficiency of combustion, elimination of water in oil storage system, and reduction of soot deposits in the furnace and convection tubes in the boiler.
□ Install soot blowers on all residual oil boiler systems.
□ Select the size of multiple-boiler installations that can be operated at 75–100 percent of rated capacity for both summer and winter load conditions.

Energy Reporting

Many companies have a hard time finding a meaningful way to measure energy savings. The experience of others is often no help since every product and process is different and requires its own method of measurement. But without a reporting system that will stand up to diagnostic review, there is no way to set targets, measure return on investment, or establish energy accountability throughout the company.

The energy audits described earlier provide a place to start. They should list in detail how much energy is being used, where it is being used, and how much it costs. The audits should also provide an energy history for every facility stretching back four or five years. All these data will help in setting a base from which to measure future savings.

Since many older plants were designed and built when energy was cheap, they have little or no submetering. Until enough metering can be installed, managers will have to use calculated numbers and/or monthly or yearly comparisons as their measurement tools.

The energy management office should design a set of detailed reporting forms that cover, for each facility, monthly energy use, energy forecasts, and energy program analysis. These forms can then be used by various departments to calculate return on investment (ROI), conduct energy survey and analysis, determine adequacy of fuel storage capacity, determine conversion requirements, determine energy's share in cost of product, evaluate and document individual plant energy programs, evaluate plant operating and maintenance programs, evaluate calculated savings on energy projects, forecast energy usage, forecast energy costs, forecast natural gas curtailment, monitor energy usage, monitor energy purchases, monitor energy costs, monitor natural gas curtailment, monitor fuel inventory levels, and set energy reduction goals.

The following reporting forms will help establish energy accountability throughout the company.

- *Monthly energy usage report:* Details monthly usage, purchases, and delivered costs by type of fuel, as well as gas curtailment and fuel inventory levels. This report should be prepared by personnel at each plant or facility.

- *Energy forecast:* Provides purchasing with estimated energy requirements for each location for the next five years. The report should cover projected usage, unit prices, and total cost by type of fuel. It should estimate usage and unit costs in both BTUs and the standard physical units of measure. If possible, projections should be by quarter for the first two years, and by year for the final three years. The report should also include actual data for the preceding years in order to form a base period for comparison.

The energy forecast helps purchasing to predict fuel costs and plan for the amount of alternative fuel and storage space needed at each location. Controllers can use the forecast to calculate return on investment for fuel conversion and energy conservation projects. And plant managers and manufacturing can use it to justify proposed energy projects.

- *Energy program analysis:* Documents, measures, and evaluates individual plant energy conservation programs. The report should include energy statistics, heating degree days, direct expense, production, building or process changes and/or additions affecting plant energy requirements, conversions, and any other projects related to energy.

This kind of reporting system ought to be a two-way street. Central management should report periodically to the people at each location on the company's progress, on the conservation record of their facility, and possibly on how well they are doing compared to other locations in the company. At 3M, for example, every plant in the program regularly receives a poster that graphically compares the energy the plant is using to the sales value of its production. All the people in the plant can see how well they are doing and know that the company is interested in their efforts. Regular feedback like this is essential for keeping the momentum of an energy program going long after the first enthusiasm has worn off.

The Challenge of Energy Management

No matter how well it is planned, an energy management program cannot succeed without the wholehearted support of top management and the full cooperation of people throughout the company. The job of energy management goes beyond conservation projects, engineering standards, and cost projections. Energy managers have to be financial analysts, who can demonstrate—in hard numbers—the potential return on investment of projects they recommend. They have to be good communicators, who can sell the benefits of energy management to people at all levels of their company. Above all, they have to be broad-ranging energy analysts, who can help their company understand the potential of alternative fuels and new technologies, likely shifts in energy prices and source of supply, and even the international policies of energy.

Good energy managers can help their companies to turn the problems of a changing energy situation into opportunities, and at the same time to become better corporate citizens of their communities.   □ *R. L. Aspenson*

COST REDUCTION

Cost reduction is considered by management to be a creative positive program aimed at profit improvement by reducing labor, materials, and manufacturing overhead cost. It is assumed that such reduction will be accomplished by systematically reevaluating and reanalyzing work methods, materials usage, manpower requirements, layouts, and basic product design.

Breaking Through the Status Quo

Many managements have tried cost reduction programs over the years with very minimal results. Managers resist the programs, which become known in operating departments as commands to chop heads or reduce costs by X percent across the board. These programs have caused managers to hoard employees, equipment, and supplies as well as to try to obfuscate details of impending windfalls and large-scale changes. Moreover, because managers are in the habit of thinking that the current levels of services, people, and associated costs are in balance with current production output, they cannot conceive that whole elements of cost may be unnecessary or that entire activities and functions may be consolidated or eliminated.

The current business climate requires significant operations improvements to restore U.S. leadership in some of our most important product areas worldwide. To achieve such improvements, it is necessary to change from status quo management to breakthrough management, a concept developed by Joseph Jurand, Fellow of the American Management Associations. To maintain the status quo, management need only: (1) choose a control point, (2) establish a unit of measure for cost and/or performance, (3) set standards, (4) measure systematically, (5) compare, and (6) judge.

To make a breakthrough in cost reduction, however, management must first be dissatisfied with the status quo and undergo an attitude change. It then becomes possible to take the actions needed: (1) identify company's chronic economic problems, (2) select important few related to chronic problems, (3) acquire new knowledge and improve diagnosis, (4) analyze change required, and in social patterns, (5) overcome resistance to change, and (6) select new mean performance goals.

Status quo management reactions can be overcome when management realizes that costs are caused by management decisions and actions. These decisions and actions occur in six general areas: product design, process design, production control and scheduling, utilization of people, maintenance of assets, and conservation of energy.

The programs that management directs in these areas will determine the level of cost the company will incur to achieve its manufacturing mission. Present costs will be reduced as dissatisfied managers make planned and deliberate changes from the present programs, people, services, structures, and systems to those that are more efficacious.

Planned Change with a Planned Action Budget

Management tools for starting such a program of deliberate change include: (1) data on labor, materials, overhead, fixed and sunk costs, (2) assignments of costs to departments and functions and special projects and/or product lines, (3) performance standards of historical or other basis to measure a production process, functional services, and/or output, (4) available time to make statistical analyses of trends, asset up-time, and so forth, (5) assessments of internal and external strengths and weaknesses as well as competitive positions for a five- to ten-year period, and (6) management acknowledgment that much of the present practices and organization may not be sacred and unalterable.

The management of costs and therefore the responsibility for planned deliberate change rests with the present management organization. Because no special team should be expected to do what is the basic responsibility of the management, a highly collaborative, multifunctional approach should be followed.

In order not to change regular information flows and reporting mechanisms, program development should be coordinated with the preparation of an annual budget. (Intensive accounting collaboration is necessary. The program, however, is a tool for manufacturing managers and not an accounting exercise.)

The key initial activity is building the plan rather than just tampering with existing, preestablished plans. In this way it is expected that innovation can occur with top-management blessing. Rather than simply summing up the expenses or the cost plans of the several units (all of which, in self-interest, compete for portions of the existing margin) a series of tradeoff decisions must be made which select the lowest net cost program for the total organization. Some functions can perform a service to manufacturing at far lower cost while some add cost without sufficient benefit in gain or margin.

Intense collaboration is required in the planning process. To achieve significant results, each manager must have a clear understanding of accountability for how each operation contributes to total performance. Open and direct communication during planning should occur. A new perception is achieved when managers realize that such planning produces a description of what "ought to be" instead of what is expected.

American managers unfortunately have been victims of their own and their consultants' analyses which establish too short planning horizons. In programs of planned deliberate change it is sometimes necessary to make expense cost investments for a change in the future. We can no longer avoid costs that are necessary to maintain positions in markets, enhance revenues, or preserve key assets.

Technique

We start such a program by establishing standards for what will be manufactured and shipped; when it will happen; what labor, materials, and supplies are required; how much time will be used by whom; who does what; and what is expected from each person and process in the operation. These activities will outline (1) the maximum levels of service or products as mandated by management, (2) the amount of inventory change to occur in the period which effects the factory production rate, (3) levels of employment of all people, and (4) machinery and equipment or process changes to be made.

The conflicts this process produces can probably be best resolved by developing a master or executive scheduling routine. This should be developed in units, not dollars, because the production activity is related to the specific units that are to be manufactured and shipped. This master schedule is a time-phased plan for materials procurement, manufacturing activity, and services of specialists. Following are the routine considerations in such a plan: (1) Determine the core of the product offering that can be planned; (2) obtain sales history and forecast; (3) schedule the appearance for shipment of new and revised product designs; (4) determine inventory changes necessary to accomplish the schedule;

(5) clearly delineate the real or achievable shop capacity, as opposed to ideal capacity; and (6) publish a time-phased schedule for revenue based on specific product being shipped.

This master schedule sets the plan for review and organizes the planned deliberate change in personnel and costs that will occur in our six cost areas. Such a time-phased plan will produce a different projected cost provided that there is sufficient dissatisfaction with the current unfavorable balance of functional services, expense, and output.

The fixed plant and equipment, investment changes, and sunk costs to be charged are an irreducible base unless assets are to be disposed of. All other costs should be determined as partly or directly variable with the units produced. The irreducible services and personnel seem best described as expenses that would be incurred if we were to shut the operation down for six months with an expectation that operations would be resumed at a minimum output level at the end of that six-month period.

Major Cost Reduction Areas

Labor, materials, and manufacturing overhead are major cost reduction areas, but mounting operating expenses (caused by inefficient or obsolete equipment and machinery) and slow inventory turnover must also be taken into account.

Labor. Direct labor costs are costs directly attributable to a product. They are frequently reduced through work methods analysis by individuals trained in time and motion study. The intent is to mechanize, eliminate, simplify, and standardize each individual operation in order to reduce costs.

Material. Direct materials costs are those directly attributable to a product. Materials costs can be lowered by instituting proper controls at key points before manufacturing begins: (1) At the time the items are designed, costs can be cut by using the techniques of value analysis and by good machine design aimed at establishing a machine capable of maintaining a desired quality level. (2) At the time of purchase, materials costs can be reduced by locating new and less expensive sources of supply and by using the techniques of value analysis. (3) At the time of receipt, good incoming inspection permits defective parts to be discovered before they reach the manufacturing area. This reduces in-process waste and permits the return of the parts to the vendor within the allowable time period.

After manufacturing operations have started, proper control of materials by the supervisor is the key to reduced materials costs. Good, close, daily supervision can reduce waste by means of clear and complete work instructions; by not permitting further processing of substandard materials; by verifying that tools and fixtures are in good repair; by salvaging reparable materials; by training new workers properly; by storing goods carefully; by discouraging pilferage; and by careful use of operating supplies.

Manufacturing overhead. Overhead costs are frequently broken down into fixed, semivariable, and variable categories so as to focus attention on specific cost areas. Fixed overhead such as taxes or depreciation does not vary directly with changes in production volume. Semivariable overhead such as supervisors' sala-ries does increase or decrease with volume but not in direct proportion. Variable overhead such as materials handlers and operating supplies changes in direct proportion to product volume. Fixed and semivariable overhead are scrutinized periodically rather than continually because they usually do not change appreci-ably from day to day. Variable overhead, on the other hand, changes rapidly and should be constantly reviewed because it offers a prime opportunity for consider-able cost savings. The responsibility for controlling these variable expenses should be in the hands of the area supervisor who is directly responsible for the costs at the point where they occur. However, the area supervisor should be held accountable only for those costs he can directly control.

Plant and equipment replacement. Establishing a replacement program re-quires a commitment from top management that an organized, systematic, and continuous replacement program is necessary and that it is an integral part of corporate policy. Top management must issue clear guidelines for the system to be used in determining plant and equipment replacement, the procedure to be followed, and the persons specifically responsible for the successful implementa-tion of the program. Some advantages of a continuous program include reduc-tion of expensive crash expenditures, lower maintenance costs, less waste, and less downtime.

Determining guidelines for replacement of equipment is a complex procedure because actual, presently known factors as well as future unknown factors must be considered. For example, predictions of the future for sales, technology, and the value of money force individual value judgments. The issue is made more complex because various methods and techniques can be used to choose between alternatives. The essential point is that, although replacement analysis is complex and is based on many unknowns, it is most necessary that a systematic mathemati-cal analysis be made, not just a guess based on past experience and intuition. Sev-eral methods for evaluating alternative proposals include the MAPI (Machinery and Allied Products Institute) method, the annual cost method, the present worth method, and the rate-of-return method. Each method has its advantages, but the one best fitted to the specific company and situation should be used.

The decade of the 1980s offers many new important considerations in capital investment for machinery and equipment, particularly in companies where prod-ucts are in midlife and maturity in the life cycle. Costs of capital and inflation of prices have affected costs of machinery and equipment. It becomes apparent that as a result of these factors, investments in increased capacity will cause increase in unit costs of product. Therefore, investments in manufacturing significantly new processes or investments in new products seem more attractive. Reconciling total corporate strategy with available capital requires collaboration between the fi-nance, manufacturing, and marketing functions now more than ever before.

Manufacturing Operations Analysis

In order for a realistic and meaningful evaluation of the overall manufacturing operation to be made, information must flow freely between the individual or team making the organizational study, the people in charge of the manufacturing process being studied, and the administrator.

Policies, procedures, and responsibilities in an organization are constantly undergoing change. For this reason, many companies make a comprehensive audit of the entire manufacturing organization before embarking on profit improvement programs. Audits can be conducted by outside consultants or corporate management, depending upon the size, circumstances, and availability of competent personnel in the company.

☐ *C. Eugene Moore* (and *John J. McCrea,* and *original author of this now substantially revised section*)

Index

Italicized names indicate contributors.

175